MW00620832

BESTSELLING AUTHOR

Ken McElroy

RETURN TO ORCHARD CANYON

A BUSINESS NOVEL

Published by:
KyleKade Press, an imprint of RDA Press LLC
Scottsdale, Arizona

Printed in the United States of America

First Edition Hardcase: 978-1-937832-82-7

Enjoyorchardcanyon.com

This book is

dedicated to my parents

and their generation.

Acknowledgements

Return to Orchard Canyon is the culmination of a lifetime of learning. It's a story that shows how a few vital ingredients, among them friends, family, money, career, dreams... can all come together and lead to a life of freedom and happiness. Or not...

I'm grateful for all who have contributed to my own lifelong journey of personal development, financial wisdom and my dreams. Without the people I've met along the way, I would not be the person I am, see the world as I do or be able to share this story. The generational characters are fiction, but their lives, circumstances and choices are real. I've known them all.

I want to sincerely thank Kathy Heasley for her incredible research, character development and especially for her ability to take many of the very basic life choices people make today and turn them into an amazing and wonderful story that touches the heart. It vividly shows that no matter where you are, a view of the past, a willingness to be present and the audacity to go for your dreams will always bring freedom.

Orchard Canyon is a real place that serves thousands of happy guests each and every year.

www.enjoyorchardcanyon.com.

CHAPTER 1

It was a necessary inconvenience. Driving two hours for what amounted to a meal and most likely polite conversation. But it was time. Way past time for a little family get-together. David felt the guilt only a son and a father can feel growing with every passing mile. *I should have made time to visit sooner. I should have stayed in touch.* A lot of shoulds.

"Why are we driving all this way again?" The question came out a bit more abruptly than Meghan wanted.

"Look, your grandfather's been asking us to drive up north to his place for a Sunday since Labor Day weekend. It's November. I think it's time we finally get up there."

"Oh yeah, the apple harvest thing at the end of the summer. A bunch of old people who always stay at the cabins in the canyon going on and on about 'how sweet the apples from the orchard are.' I mean, big deal. It's an apple. Apples are everywhere. Is today going to be like that?"

"I don't know. I don't think there's anything going on at the resort this weekend, but I'm bracing myself for anything. You know your grandfather. He might be 82, but he is a businessman and a bit of a social butterfly. The resort he created where I grew up is loved by the people who visit it every year. When he's with all those folks, like at the apple harvest festival, he's kind of like a celebrity. He mixes it up with them and doesn't have a care in the world. And say what you want about those 'old' people—they were having a pretty good time with my dear ol' dad."

David clung to those words as he drove north on I-17 toward Sedona, Arizona, to his dad's house, his own childhood home nestled deep in the canyon on Oak Creek. What was once the family's home is now Orchard Canyon Resort, a charming 12-acre getaway with just 18 cabins and surroundings that attract countless people—many of whom are now Ron's friends—from around the nation. How could his dad not have a care in the world? He's running a resort *and* an orchard *and* a restaurant *and* dealing with all these people. The place takes a lot of care and maintenance. Maybe when we saw him last September it was on a good day, when the demands were few.

David couldn't grasp it. His own life was anything but carefree. Here he was, 57, divorced, spending time—part time—with his only daughter, Meghan, who had one more year before she left for college. She'd soon be gone and David was feeling the regret of missing her life. Where did the time go? Her childhood, her teens, now it's her senior year. David and his wife divorced and Meghan lives in a historic district of Phoenix with Susan, about twenty miles from the Scottsdale mini-mansion they all shared years ago and where David still lives.

Glancing in his driver's side mirror, David could see the left lane was clear for the moment and veered over. He and Meghan were at the part of the drive where you just climb, climb, climb, climb from the lower deserts to the higher elevation of northern Arizona. It's easily a 5,000-foot change in elevation. Vehicles hauling any weight struggle to make that climb, and David carefully passed three trucks and a motor home that were burning a lot of fuel to make it up the steep grade.

Once he got past the road hazards—*You just never know with trucks*, he thought—his mind went back to trying to make sense of his week and his life. He spent his entire career in banking, gave his weekends, put his family second, if truth be told, only to find himself as of two days ago, a casualty of his company's latest merger. How many mergers, how many deals had he brought together for that place? Busted his ass, gave up holidays and school plays and Meghan's soccer games and family dinners. He even poured through the analytics on this latest deal and the numbers looked good. But then, with no warning, he's out! *Laid off. Laid off! Who the hell did I piss off?* He was driving numb.

"So what do you think we'll be having to eat?" Meghan, whose eyes were still glued to Instagram on her phone, attempted to break into his internal dialog. "It better not be something disgusting because I'm not eating it if it is." She got no response. "If it's like broccoli and meat on a bone, we're stopping at McDonald's on the way home. Just warning you." Meghan then peered out the window, then back down to her iPhone, then back out the window. "Is there a cell tower somewhere around here? I only have two bars."

The drive up from the lower deserts of Arizona onto the Mogollon Rim looked almost surreal in the morning. The light cast long shadows from the saguaro cactus dotting the mountains near Black Canyon, the tan earth looking reddish gold in the morning light, and the bit of frost that tipped the sagebrush as their car crested the rim. "It's freezing up here," Meghan said, and pulled her jean jacket around her.

"Well, it's a pretty big altitude change. Looks like it's just 43 degrees here." David said. It was 70 in Scottsdale where they lived. The rangeland looked a little tired and depleted, she thought. Meghan had no idea that her opinion of the scenery whizzing by was not too far off from how her dad was feeling about his own life at the moment. And how it was passing by almost as quickly.

"Hey, before we get to Orchard Canyon ..." David paused. "I'm not going to tell your grandfather about my job situation. I'm just telling you so you don't say something. I mean, it's just a matter of time before I'm back into the grind." How humiliating to have to bring this up to his daughter, and how unsure he was if what he just said was true. How much worse if his father knew. "I just want to make sure. It's a private thing."

Meghan interrupted, "I wouldn't say anything," a little surprised. "Do you think I'm a blabbermouth?" In truth, she might have said *something*. What was the big deal anyway? There are other jobs; how hard is it to find another job? Is it some big secret?

"No, you're not a blabbermouth. I just want to make sure we keep the developments of last week to ourselves. When I'm ready to tell him—if I'm ever ready to tell him—I'll do it. Like I said, this is very temporary." Truth was, David had no intention of telling his dad that he was a midlife unemployed banker. How does that happen? He did everything for that damn company. *Bastards. Just like that, "Thank you, but I'm sorry to tell you ..."* The anger and the hurt began to swell in him again. *...We have to let you go."*

David had been a loyal company man, always figuring that the company and the people he worked with for years would protect him. That wasn't the company anymore. The new management came in and they didn't know him from Adam. Didn't want to know him from Adam. All his relationships — though there weren't that many — were gone. The new guys at the top brought along their friends, and the pawns, like David who got the company to where it was, were dead weight. *Pawns, That's really what I was, wasn't I?* he thought. *A professional pawn, completely removable from my company's chess board.*

A little more than an hour after they left Phoenix, they were winding their way through the red rock country nearing Sedona. There's something magical about the place the first time and every time you visited. "I'm always in awe of those red rocks," David said, interrupting himself from his own self-deprecating thoughts. Even though David grew up near here and couldn't wait to graduate and start college at Arizona State University, in Tempe, coming back and traversing the scenic byways always gave him a peaceful feeling. Coming back so seldom made the scenery even more striking. His nerves calmed for the remainder of the trek, until he got through town and hit Route 89A. From the moment he made that right turn onto that narrow road through Oak Creek Canyon, his tension was back. "Well, we're almost there," which came out a little ominous and not quite as positive as he intended. He wasn't ready to face his dad.

He slowed down and took the left-hand turn, hidden amongst the trees, onto the little access road of the resort. It had been a rainy month so Oak Creek was flowing strong. David's tires carefully crossed through the rushing water of the creek and began the final mile up to the resort. As he turned into the stone driveway of the main house, now the Orchard Canyon Resort lodge, Meghan looked up from her iPhone. There wasn't any cell service anyway, so why not look out the window? That road surface always made such a distinctive sound with the rubber on gravel. It was like a popping noise, as the random stones flew back from the tires. To him that sound always signified he wasn't in the city anymore. It signified being out of his element. It used to mean failure because to him, the big city of Phoenix was his next stop in life. But now he didn't need the stones on the rock drive to remind him of failure. He had plenty reminders of his own.

They approached the main house and, not surprisingly, it looked just like it always had. Same dark log-beam front porch. Same heavy wood door. Same curtains visible through the windows. The shadows appeared longer, more severe, in the morning autumn sun that always took a long time to make its way into the canyon. It was colder, too, with the canyon walls rising up on both sides. And the greenness from Labor Day, the optimism of the summer foliage, now lay dead on the ground. The scent of autumn, of decaying leaves, was rich in the air. David had a feeling of despair as he slowed down in the drive and pulled into one of the guest parking spaces. He threw the car into park and did his best to shake off his earlier thoughts.

Looking at his daughter with false enthusiasm, he said, "Okay, let's get this show on the road."

"You mean over with?" Meghan absent-mindedly said as she shifted her gaze to the front window, her elbow leaning on the door and her head resting in her hand. Meghan was sensitive and could pick up on what surely must have been in the air: dread. She was right. Get this over with.

Letting that comment slide, the two climbed out of David's black BMW, closed the doors, and, through force of habit, David pressed the lock button. Then unlocked it. *No need for that here,* he remembered. The cabins the guests stayed in didn't even have locks on the doors. *It's a step back to another time*, David thought.

Meghan grabbed her purse, her long scarf, and more importantly her phone and began walking toward the front door that was now the reception area for the resort. She was lagging behind her dad. "You coming, Meghan?" She picked up her pace.

David approached the front door and looked down to see that same wood latch mechanism that was part of that house when he was a kid. *Home is where the heart is,* a sign said. *Is it?* he thought. For him and the life he led, home was where he slept, and not much more. Just as he began pondering what home was or wasn't and thinking, *Who in this day and age doesn't have a real lock on a door?* it flew open.

"David! Meghan! Come in, come in! I'm so happy to see you!"

Chapter 2

CHAPTER 2

Ronald Reynolds, lifelong fruit grower, also answered to the names Ron, Dad and your grandfather. He really wished there was a Gramps thrown in there, but the fact was, he and Meghan just didn't have that kind of relationship. They didn't know each other that well. He aimed to fix that.

For eight years now, David and he both lived in the same part of the world. Ron on the family farm along Oak Creek and David a few hours south in Scottsdale near Phoenix. The drive to northern Arizona used to feel much farther away, David thought, but as Phoenix has grown and the freeways got bigger, it made getting to his childhood home much easier and faster. The very land where the family home stood in the Sedona/Oak Creek Canyon area used to be one of many in the region with apple, peach and pear orchards. Now it was one of the last.

Chapter 2

Ron will tell you it's because people sold their land to developers who build too many houses and too many stores. That was his point of view. But even with more houses and more stores, Sedona was still very much a small town compared to Phoenix.

Ron grew up here. The son of a farmer who was the son of a pioneer who made the trek west from somewhere in the heartland of America. Hard work and working with your hands was bred into the family. Well, bred in until Ron's son David. David was a hard worker, it was just a different kind of hard. He worked hard at an office job, and before that a different office job and before that a different office job, about five or six times over in his 30-year career. Hard work didn't mean putting in a good day's labor with sweat and grit, then sitting down to dinner with the family. It meant commuting, working all day, missing lunch, eating a quick burger from Wendy's at about 3:00, then getting home too late to eat more than whatever was left on the stove from dinner. Often pizza, or on a good night, maybe some cold pasta.

Born in 1935, Ron was the son of Eleanor and Fred, two determined, self-made success stories. They were the ones who took a family orchard with a house, which grew enough for them to live on then sell what was left to the community, and turned it into a business. They purchased more land when it came up for sale, another orchard down the road. Now they owned 12 acres. They invested in the future, which, given the industrialization going on in the Eastern cities, meant they looked for ways to do the same thing on the farm. Improvement and efficiency along with scale. Getting bigger meant getting more efficient, and that was good.

Working was a way of life for young Ron. From the time he could pick up a farm implement — which was about the same time he learned to pick up a spoon — his work life began. In essence, if you can feed yourself, you can work. That's the way it was on the Reynolds' orchard. Down the road, the Sauer's farm in Cottonwood and the Littleston's ranch beyond that all operated the same way. The Sauers and the Littlestons, they had a bunch of kids who all worked. That was the way it was. Fred and Eleanor had only one child, Ron, and a few hands, who picked apples, pressed cider, and kept the place up. Eleanor kept the house, raised Ron, did the canning, and sold preserves and pies at the corner stand. Work started before dawn and often lasted until after dark. There were no days off. Something always needed tending to. For Fred and Eleanor, it didn't feel like pressure; it felt like simply living.

Chapter 2

But, as America continued along its inevitable shift from farm to city, Eleanor believed that the future for her only son, Ron, wasn't here. The world was changing and life on the farm, while noble and "what Reynolds do," wasn't the life she had in mind for the son she adored. She saw how smart he was, how good he was. "Ron, you are a smart boy. When you grow up you are going to do great things," she would promise him. She was really promising herself.

Fred had no time for or interest in Eleanor's aspirations for her son, of wanting something more for him than just being part of the family business. It became a sore spot from time to time in the family. "That boy should go to a better school, Fred. He's smarter than the rest of the kids. He can do more. He can be more!" Eleanor exclaimed one evening. Twelve-year-old Ron was listening from inside while his parents were talking on the front porch. They thought he was in the barn. But he heard it all.

"Smarter than the other kids? Kids are kids, Ellie. They need to know what they need to know. That's it. Then they learn the things to make a living right here on the job. They learn to farm, to raise chickens, grow and press apples, to repair and maintain equipment, to buy and sell. Those are the things that boy needs."

Ron sat quietly thinking to himself that he liked the farm, the canyon, and the creek. He loved all the places on it to hide and think and explore. He liked farm work, taking care of animals and even repairing stuff. *But what if there is something more?* He'd never been to Phoenix, the biggest city in the Southwest. *There is a college near there.* He wondered ...

Life on the farm happened day-by-day, week-by-week and eventually year-by-year. Talk of Ron going to a better school never went anywhere. A brief discussion about college didn't go anywhere either. Fred simply closed the two-minute discourse with, "College? What do you mean, college? Who's going to help me here, Eleanor? You? Forget it."

Ron didn't miss not going to college, but he never forgot his father's words. One day—he was all of 16—he got his nerve up to ask his father, "So, Pop, I think I'd like to maybe go to college one day."

"Son, that's the kind of place for people who don't have nothing to do. We got a lot to do here. I need you here. You can forget college." And that was the end of it ... for Ron.

Ron fell in love with a local girl and married his wife Mary in 1956. They attended the same small Sedona High School and Ron was three years older. They had their first dance at the county stock show. And their first official date followed shortly after. It wasn't long before they got married and had three children.

Right from the start, Ron was determined to give each of them the opportunity to go to college. For all his days running the orchard, the resort, and everything else in the canyon, he felt he had a good life .... but what if he had gone to college? He wondered what else he might have been able to do. Who knows? He may have ended up right where he was, except with a degree. Regardless, that life was not open to him and he vowed things would be different for his own kids. Ron encouraged college all through their upbringing, and all three went to universities.

Mary didn't go to college either. She fell in love instead. Then the babies came and her responsibilities were to the family and to Ron. She was happy being the matriarch of all that was Orchard Canyon. It gave her all the time and opportunity to do the things that she loved. Nurturing children, cooking, welcoming guests at the resort, entertaining, managing the restaurant, and keeping the books. Yes, Mary was the bookkeeper with a natural gift for numbers. That's where David got his financial genes. Sometimes he would help his mother keep track of the resort's weekly earnings.

Both David's younger brother and sister became business owners living north of Sedona in Flagstaff. Michael got into real estate investing in Arizona and was branching out to Colorado. Kathi started a non-traditional private school for K-12 and was getting ready to open her second location. Both were married and both had children. They'd stop down to the canyon on their travels since work took them to Sedona rather often.

Ron told all three of his children that they were going to grow up strong and smart. On the day David was born, Ron looked at him and said, "You're going to be the first one in our family to go to college." It was his birth wish for every one of his kids, and he meant it, reciting the same birthday wish every year with increased zeal. He became more and more convinced the way to get ahead was by getting a college degree. And it seemed he was right. All three of his children became successful professionals.

It seems like yesterday to Ron. He would be walking in from the barn and the cider shed and spot his oldest son.

"David, are your chores finished?"

"Yes, sir."

"How about your homework," he asked even more sternly.

"Almost," David replied.

"Well, get to it then!"

That's pretty much how it went in the Reynolds' house in the 1960s, '70s, and '80s leading up to David's acceptance and scholarship to Arizona State University. Ron had achieved his dream for his first-born. With a college degree, life would be perfect for his son David.

Now here David stood, at the front door, his father beaming at both him and his granddaughter. They had the perfect life, it seemed. David, successful, beautiful daughter in tow. Sure there was the divorce, but we do live in the 21st century. As much as Ron hated to see David and Susan split, it happens. At least it is amicable. *Susan, she is another one,* Ron thought in a momentary flash as he saw the two. *Another ASU graduate, highly accomplished in business and now a business owner herself. I bet her parents are so proud of her. She's a wonderful girl. Just like my son is a wonderful son.*

Ron ushered the two in the door, "What took you so long? I was beginning to think you might not be coming." As David and Meghan walked in, Ron picked up a vibe from his son. David seemed distant and he wondered why. Ron always wanted more for David than he could have gotten in the canyon. But he couldn't shake the feeling that maybe life for David wasn't so good, and that maybe life in the orchard, in the canyon, was a pretty good life after all.

"Oh, geez, Dad. We just got a bit of a late start this morning and everything took longer than expected. You know how that goes. I should have called. Sorry," David said, immediately feeling bad for dragging his own feet to get here. He just didn't feel up to this visit. He knew there'd be questions he didn't want to answer. Not probing, nosy questions. Just conversation that he knew would be ... uncomfortable.

"And you, Meghan! Look at you, getting prettier every day, growing up," he cheerily said as he greeted her with a hug and a kiss on the forehead. "It's been forever since I've seen you. And we all live just up the road." Ron let his thoughts escape and instantly he knew the words he said aloud sounded like a guilt trip. He didn't mean it that way. "What I'm saying is, it's just great to have you both here. C'mon, let's go to the house so I can show you what I have in the kitchen."

As they walked from the old lodge across the orchard to the residence that Ron called home, it was as if nothing had changed. They walked through the entry hallway, past the living room, complete with the old family couch, Ron's favorite velour recliner, and a second-generation flat-screen TV that was 10 years old but still looked new. It blared CNN virtually all day long. Even though Ron was in excellent shape, maybe his hearing wasn't what it used to be. "TV's a little loud. I like to be able to hear it from the kitchen," Ron said as he lowered the volume. Ron's hearing was fine, as was everything else. He was as healthy as the proverbial horse. The fresh air and physical work had a way of keeping you young.

As they made their way to the kitchen, both David and Meghan felt like they had stepped back in time. The place looked no different than it must have looked in the '60s when David was born. Same tile walls, same tile countertop, same cabinets and old-fashioned faucets, punctuated with a few modern conveniences like a microwave oven and an espresso machine. While in the army, Ron spent a year in Italy and brought his love of good coffee home with him.

What's with the separate controls for the hot and the cold water in the kitchen sink? I never noticed that before. It's so weird, Meghan thought as she stood near the sink and recalled the never-ending shopping and continual discussions about sinks, cabinets, appliances, countertops, when her parents completely redid the kitchen several years ago. Even though she thought the whole thing was an inconvenience, the remodel process made her aware of design and now she's the first to admit she kinda' likes having the newest and the best at her dad's and in her own home with her mom. Last year Susan took her historic house in central Phoenix and updated it.

David was the same way. He liked the best of everything and had achieved it in most areas of his life. All those niceties might not be fully paid for yet, but he has them. He was not foreign to using home equity loans to buy what he wanted. *With house values going up so quickly in Scottsdale*, he thought, *what was the harm? That's why you buy a house, right? The appreciation.*

Ron eagerly walked over to the counter and picked up a Ball canning jar with a shiny gold lid. Holding it proudly, "So what do you think of this? Mrs. James—you remember her don't you, David? She's Jeanie's mom." Then interrupting himself, "Did you know that Jeanie—she's now Jean—is a bigwig on Wall Street in New York? She works with money like you do. They're so proud of her. Anyway, Mrs. James brought over these peaches she canned from this season. I've been wanting to have them with some vanilla ice cream, but I thought I'd wait for you two to visit. That's our dessert. Doesn't that sound good?"

Chapter 2

"It does, Dad," said David, wondering exactly how long his dad's been waiting to have those peaches. Has it really just been since August? David had to cancel or decline at least four invitations to visit over the last few months. Something always got in the way. Most of the time, he had work commitments and the rest of the time, he was too tired from work commitments. It was just easier to grab something to go and bring it home on the way from the office. *The office. Yeah, I don't have an office anymore.* The thought interrupted his guilt trip. "Sorry if I made you delay enjoying those peaches. They look great. You should have just dug in."

"No, it's okay, it's okay. So I hope you like baked potatoes, home-smoked ham, and Brussels sprouts. I know you do, David; how about you, young lady?" Ron asked, suddenly directing his attention at Meghan who was still blown away by how oddly the faucet was mounted on the wall OVER the sink, not ON the sink. It actually was kind of cool retro.

"That will be fine. Sure," Meghan said. "Um ... is there any cell service or Wi-Fi here?" She didn't address her grandfather directly because she didn't know what to call him. She just didn't see him that often, so she didn't feel comfortable calling him "Gramps" or "Grandpa," and "Grandfather" sounded so formal. So she just didn't ever call him anything.

She hoped he didn't notice. Should she ask, "What do you want me to call you?" There were no other kids around whose lead she could follow, so it was always awkward.

"Yes, there's Wi-Fi here ..." Ron said, but David interrupted.

"Brussels sprouts will be more than fine, Dad, and Meghan, give the phone a rest, okay?" said David, recovering a bit from both Meghan's unenthusiastic answer and her request. He knew that the Brussels sprouts they were going to eat his dad grew. The ham, his dad raised and smoked. The potatoes, he planted and dug up. Food wasn't just food. To Dad, food was life. *There was no such thing as GMO foods. Just organic, farm-raised food the way it should be,* David thought.

"So how are things with you, David? You getting along? I know it's been over a year since Susan moved out, but there still must be some settling in," Ron asked, hoping for a positive response. Maybe that's why David didn't seem present. He's still getting his life together after the divorce.

"No, things are good, they're good. It is nice to have Meghan every other weekend—how about it Meghan, we have fun, right? You have friends near my house." Meghan nodded. "But yeah, we've settled into our weekend routine. Of course, Susan isn't far away, so we help each other." And then avoiding any more talk about personal stuff, he added "Hey Dad, Meghan is a senior this year!"

"Well, by gosh, I can't believe it," he added, as he ushered everyone to the front porch to enjoy the first sunlight making its way above the canyon walls. "I just love this time of day and this view. The sun cresting the canyon, the light just hitting the orchard. The blue sky and the trees, still a bit dewy. Reminds me of how your mother used to love this time of day. Makes me think of her. She'll be gone seven years here coming up."

"Yeah, I know. It doesn't seem that long ago. You're doing okay, right?"

"Oh, I'm fine. I've got this beautiful place, the resort and all the nice people who visit here—there's always something I need to do around this place—I've got neighbors, good friends who look out for me and I look out for them. And I've got security. I don't owe anything to anyone. What more could I ask for?"

What more could I ask for? David thought.

"And of course I have you both. Cheers!" The three toasted with some nice warm coffee and hot chocolate.

CHAPTER 3

Meghan took a sip of the hot chocolate and wrapped her scarf around her neck. The sun was up but it hadn't warmed the air yet. Living in Arizona, being born and raised in Scottsdale, Meghan didn't really have a concept of what cold really felt like—aside from trips to Park City, Utah, skiing with her parents and her friends. *That could be cold,* she thought as she pulled her sleeves over her hands just a bit, but not so much that she couldn't hold her iPhone.

Meghan had less than a year to go before leaving for college. On one hand, she couldn't wait. On the other hand, she had no idea what she wanted to do. The whole idea of the future was not a fully-formed concept or maybe just not as "futuristic" as it would be in the mind of an adult. To Meghan, the future was next weekend's football game, the test that's happening Thursday, and tomorrow's trip to the hair salon—she was promised highlights if she aced her last calculus test. The "future" wasn't what she wanted to do with her life. It was a week from now.

Meghan was a blessing when she was born. The operative words being "when she was born." David and Susan weren't sure they wanted kids when they first got married; they were both completely into each other and their careers. They were entry-level, both working for a big bank. At age 28 they married and barely even took time for a honeymoon. About six years into their marriage, the maternal pang hit Susan: "I think we should start a family."

"A family? Seriously?" asked David, a bit in disbelief. They were in their mid-30's, living a relatively uncomplicated life, and working their tails off. *Work hard, play hard. That's what my boss wants*, thought David. And he did both. Susan mostly just worked hard.

Women weren't really included in the play part of that age-old, good ol' boy equation. *How am I supposed to ever get the VP positions if I'm not invited to the party?*, thought Susan, who knew the party was the golf course, and how much business happened there. "Maybe it's time for me to be a mom," she said. "For us to be parents, David. You a dad!" She attempted some enthusiasm, but could see the shock on David's face.

"Okay ... when exactly were you thinking of starting this family?" David asked, tiptoeing carefully to see just how much Susan had thought this through. If her answer was, "Oh, I don't know. I was just thinking about it," David would be able to breathe a sigh of relief. That meant she was just thinking out loud. Which really meant nothing. He'd have time to point out how free and awesome their life was and why they wouldn't want to mess it up.

If she said something like, "Well, I'd like to start this month. In fact, tonight because I'm at my most fertile," David knew she was way ahead of him. He knew he would have no recourse unless he wanted a battle. And after the business trip he had just been on, working all day to integrate a new bank acquisition his company made and then late night dinners and drinks, he just didn't want to go there. A quiet, normal night at home. That's all he wanted. He braced himself for the answer.

"Well, tonight, actually," Susan said with a coy smile. "I promise you'll enjoy it," she tried to lighten the mood. "I mean, David, don't freak out. People never get pregnant the first time, so don't worry. You'll have plenty of time to get used to the idea."

Chapter 3

Truth was, David and Susan did have plenty of time to get used to the idea. Between their work schedules, downright fatigue from long days, disagreements about the whole idea of kids, the intermittent anger that went with it, and the stress of not conceiving, it took David and Susan five years to get pregnant. And of course by that time, they pretty much had abandoned the whole idea.

David's career took him on the road a good bit and Susan became more and more despondent with her career. She felt overlooked and under-appreciated and began toying with the idea of doing something on her own. Why not? The corporate world of finance was not getting her anywhere. She saw herself as a middle management lifer and knew she had way more to offer. *If my supervisors don't want to see it, their loss*, she thought. But what business would she start? There were many unknowns, so in the meantime Susan drove to the office every morning and back home at night.

The day that Susan realized she was pregnant, she couldn't believe it. "We only did it once this month! How is that possible?" she asked herself as she looked at the pregnancy test stick in the mirror. Part of her was happy, another part scared, and another part wondering what she was going to tell David. And when? He wouldn't be back until Sunday and it was Tuesday. "I have to keep this to myself for five days?" It was a lament, not a question.

When David learned of the news, he immediately started doing the math. *I'm 39 now. The baby will be born when I'm 40. By the time he or she goes to college I'll be 57. Fifty-seven!* he said in his head. What came out of his mouth, though was simply, "Wow, that's amazing news, Sus. Are you happy?" the uplift at the end a deliberate attempt to conjure up some excitement in himself and ward off his fear. It didn't work.

More numbers. David couldn't help himself. *My salary is $94,000 a year, plus a bonus; Susan's is $72,000 a year. We have saved virtually nothing other than my 401(k) and her 401(k) and I don't even know how much we have now. The market ups and downs, does anyone really open those statements? What if Susan decides to stay at home? We'd have to talk about that. No, that's not an option. There's no way we could afford that. But then how would we pay for daycare? How much does that* cost? *We are just making it as it is. And how much is baby food? Are diapers expensive? They have to be. Raising a baby has to take a ton of diapers!* David's analytical brain was running way ahead of him and at lightning speed.

Susan replied unconvincingly, “Yeah, I’m really happy. I mean, I’m a little scared, too. This is a big deal, you know.”

“Oh yeah, I know,” David said with a tad too much energy and recognizing full well that Susan had no idea just how colossal this “big deal” had grown in David’s mind. It was the size of a whale and rapidly growing to the size of a T. rex. He had to be ghost white. “So what are we going to do?” asked David, not even sure what he was asking. He just knew he needed something other than “I’m pregnant” dangling in the air. He needed some future reassurance.

“What do you mean ‘What are we going to do?’ We’re going to have a baby!” said Susan a bit defensively. “I thought you’d be a little happier about it, frankly.”

“No, I’m happy. It’s just settling in.” Then, in a shallow recovery attempt, “And I didn’t mean, ‘What are we going to do?’ like ‘Are we going to have it?’ I meant like, ‘Are you going to keep working? Are we going to need day care?’ That kind of stuff, Sus. No, I’m happy,” both his voice and his gaze trailed off.

“Well, God, David, I haven’t thought of any of that kind of stuff. I mean talk about the cart before the horse. The diaper before the baby butt! We have a long way to go before that. And I don't know what I'll do. I'm not getting anywhere at the bank, clearly," Susan lingered on that last word. "Maybe it'll be an opportunity to do something on my own. You know I've been thinking about it. ... you know," with a shoulder shrug. "I don't know ..." Susan's voice trailed off and she looked away. She felt some tears coming.

David, who was now looking out over his dad's orchard 18 years later, of course didn't know everything Susan was thinking, and didn't know about her tearful ending to that first conversation. David had left the room by then. But it's amazing how quickly the mind can take you back. All this flashback action from Ron commenting to Meghan, "Pretty soon, you'll be going to college, young lady. Where does the time go?"

David was feeling the same fear now that he had felt when he learned he was going to be a dad. Completely unprepared, not in the best circumstances financially, and worried to death. His silence now was exactly the same as it had been 18 years ago, except he couldn't walk away. At least when his mind was racing, his mouth didn't function. That had always worked in his favor.

"Boy, and is college expensive these days! Do you know how much it costs to go to a university?" Ron directed his comment to David this time. David took it as code for his father implying, "I hope you've been saving for this, David."

David wasn't going there. See, this was exactly why he didn't want to come to dinner. Why he wanted to make up an excuse and cancel. Trapped! These were the kinds of conversations he didn't need right now. *Of course I'm not prepared! Who's prepared? Who can afford to be prepared? I just lost my damn job,* he screamed in his head.

"Hey, Meghan! Do you see that right over there?" David asked changing the subject, fully diverting the conversation and attempting a recovery as quickly as possible. He looked for anything, —anything—to get his dad off the talk of college and finances.

"See what?" Meghan replied barely looking up from her phone. She was in the heat of a text conversation with a girlfriend about one of the Kardashians. Apparently she found a pocket of cell service. Even though she couldn't care less about self-centered celebrities, they're still kinda' interesting.

"Could you look up from your phone for just a minute, Meghan? You're missing the deer right over there."

"I'm pretty sure there are a lot of deer around here, Dad. It's northern Arizona," she said a little smartly.

David whispered, "Very funny, but no, check it out there's three of them right over there. Amazing." They both stared in relative (albeit, for Meghan, brief) awe.

Ron, of course stared in awe, too. And in disbelief that these two, who have lived in Arizona all their lives, were making such a fuss over the buck and two does that forage every morning in the orchard. He practically had them named. He thought how sad it is that most people, including David and Meghan, miss out having nature this close in their lives. What else have they missed? He started to get a picture of their life and just how far removed his family had come from the wisdom of the land and the farm. One generation removed. And now the next.

"Yeah, they're cool," said Meghan looking up and then down to quickly respond "OMG, U R 2 funny" to the latest beep on her phone.

Chapter 4

CHAPTER 4

"Who's hungry?" Ron asked. By now it was past noon and the whole canyon was washed in sunlight. He clapped his hands, "C'mon, let's go in and have a nice Sunday dinner. I know you said you have to get back later today, so we'll eat a little early. It's starting to warm up a bit, isn't it? Pretty soon we'll go on a walk around the place. I built a few more cabins so we can accommodate a few more visitors." Ron continued, "I'm turning into a regular Conrad Hilton. Meghan, he was the founder of Hilton Hotels. You've heard of Hilton Hotels, right? You need to come up and stay the whole weekend."

"Sounds good, Dad. But I know how much you have going on, and me too. Plus I'm sure Michael and Kathi come by and keep you company a lot. Getting away for them isn't as tough as it is for me." David didn't really want to think beyond this one uncomfortable afternoon or the fact that he hadn't seen or really thought about any of them—his father, his brother, or his sister—in months. Work was all he thought about. *Let's get through this one, how 'bout it?* Somehow his brother and sister, he believed, felt more at home here. How would he know? He barely talked to them either.

Ron pointed to the table and chairs facing the kitchen to guide David and Meghan to their seats. It was the dinette set from when David was a kid. Nothing fancy, circa 1968, with a Formica® top and stainless steel legs. The chairs matched and had been reupholstered. Ron remembered rips in the vinyl back in the '70s. These were definitely redone but with the same kind of vinyl he remembered sticking to as a kid. For years, David could never figure out why his mom kept this old table and chairs. They could have afforded something newer and they had a nice dining room set that was from Ron's family. It came with the farm. David could see its deep mahogany wood through the hallway and the crocheted lace doilies in their historic places. *Clearly that room doesn't get used much, maybe Christmas, Easter, Thanksgiving, the usual. Some things never change*, David thought. *So grateful we're not in there. That's a tougher room than this one.*

The table they were sitting at was now no longer an outdated relic, but to today's 20- and 30-somethings, a hip, vintage mid-century modern treasure. David's friends had knock-offs of these tables in their game rooms. They called them charming and retro. "Cool table," Meghan said as she walked into the room. She was just getting to the age where she was beginning to notice cool stuff. Blame it on the remodels she lived through or saw on reality TV. Or give credit to it, depending. To David, it was the former. Meghan's new-found eye for cool and her expensive taste were both costing him more money.

Ron said, "I'll sit there," pointing to his usual seat. David followed suit, taking his childhood seat. He felt 10. Meghan filed into the only other chair with silverware in front of it. She didn't have a "seat" to speak of. "Let me get a little food going,"said Ron.

"Dad, hey, let me help you," David said, leaping up from his chair. The old trick, being in motion, helping out was far better than being a sitting duck at a dinner table. In helper mode, the conversation can spiral around the activities of the moment—carrying bowls, turning off the stove, finding salt and pepper shakers—not the past or the future, neither of which David wanted to talk about. "Meghan, do you want to make room on the table?" Ron and David opened the oven and pulled out the ham, baked potatoes, and the roasted Brussels sprouts. "This looks and smells great, Dad."

"Well, it is great. Wait 'til you taste this ham, Meghan. There's nothing like it." Ron made the contrast in his mind between this ham he smoked himself and the processed hams people buy at grocery stores. David was contrasting it to the ham sandwich he had at the airport a few weeks ago. And Meghan, she was looking at the whole meal apprehensively. It was like an exotic dinner from a foreign country. In a way, that wasn't far off. All the food was on a plate, not out of a box or a bag. It was fresh out of the oven and piping hot, not pulled out from under a heat lamp.

As Ron carved the ham and gave everyone hearty helpings, he asked, "Meghan, what are some of your favorite foods? You're getting kind of grown up now. Are you going to try the Brussels sprouts?"

"Um, I think I'll pass on those. Food I like? I'm kind of into a chicken fingers phase," Meghan replied, peering across the table looking at the dish filled with the green mini-cabbages.

"Let's say a blessing," Ron took the lead and Meghan looked at her dad trying to figure out what she was supposed to do. Saying grace wasn't something she was used to. "Thank you, Lord, for this day, the gift of David and Meghan here with me, the wonderful bounty of Orchard Canyon that created this meal, and, of course, please bless the people we love and all those in need. Amen."

Meghan picked up her fork and took a small bite of the farm-raised and cured ham. She was pleasantly surprised. It tasted amazing. "This is really really good," she looked up smiling and thinking, *Where has this been all my life?* Everything about this meal, the food, the aromas, the dishes the glasses, the forks and knives were a departure from her norm. She was more accustomed to paper cups from Starbucks and plastic spoons. David said nothing about her not wanting to try the Brussels sprouts. He was thrilled she liked the ham, given how narrow her palate was. He blamed Susan and himself for that. *Who has time to bake ham and prepare fresh vegetables? Chicken fingers, mac and cheese, pizza, Chips Ahoy! for dessert—that's dinner to us.*

"Chicken fingers! I didn't know chickens had fingers," said Ron, laughing maybe a little too heartily at his own joke. "What are chicken fingers?" he asked, still laughing, his eyes and face showing a full smile.

Meghan couldn't help but flash a small smile at that one and roll her eyes in Ron's direction. "They're pieces of fried chicken. You dip them in sauces and eat them," explained Meghan. "You've never had chicken fingers?" She was slightly shocked. "You're missing out."

"What do you think of these potatoes, honey," David carefully coaxed her toward politeness while shooting her a look that said, *Eat that potato!*

"It's good. Potatoes are on my list."

"Well, I'm glad potatoes are on your list," Ron teased.

The three ate in awkward silence for what seemed like far too long although it was probably just a minute, not even two. David scoured his brain for something safe to say, something that wouldn't lead to something else he didn't want to talk about. He had nothing.

Ron filled the gap, "So let's pick up on what we were talking about earlier. Meghan, what are you thinking about for college? Got any schools in mind?" As much as David hated to admit it, he was glad Meghan was in the hot seat and not him. But to his surprise, she took the question in stride.

"Umm ... I'm not sure. I mean, maybe ASU, but I think I really want to go to UCLA. Yeah, I'm not totally sure." Every time Meghan would bring up UCLA, David would began calculating in-state versus out-of-state tuition. "May I have another piece of ham?" Meghan asked. Ron was all too happy to oblige.

"Well, have you given some thought to what you want to be?" David asked. "That would play a role in your decision about a university." A big part of him wanted her to go into finance or accounting. Even though *he* was out of a job at the moment, those majors provided a great foundation for just about anything a person wanted to do in life. You can't go wrong knowing how to make and manage money, but then looking at his own life he wondered, *Maybe that's not entirely true.*

"I say don't rush these kids about what they want to be," Ron said after finishing a bite of ham. "It's not like when I was your age, Meghan, and there were what seemed like fewer job options, compared to today. Then, you could be a teacher or a welder or a farmer or a businessman or a fireman or a doctor. It was simple. Today, there are so many different jobs, complex jobs in complex industries. Businesses of all kinds. How can someone your age begin to know what you want to be?" Ron asked, not realizing that David believed everyone should be like he was at that age. He saw bankers around town who had the nicest houses and cars; they seemed rich. He wanted that for himself, so he followed the money. Isn't that the way it worked?

"Yeah, I'm not sure what I want to be. I like math, I like English. I like history. I like a lot of stuff. But I'm not sure what I want to do." Thinking for a bit, Megan continued "I also really like how mom has her own business. That's pretty cool. And her company is fun. I mean people seem like they're having fun there. I worked there during the summer last year, and I go in sometimes when she needs extra help. I don't know. Maybe something with social media. I like that."

David kept his head down, *Social media. Is that really even a job?* he thought.

"Well, I say, go with something you like. Look at me. I wanted to go to college, that really was my dream. But, in those days, it wasn't what regular people did. My mother and father needed me on the farm, so I did what was expected of me. I stayed on the farm." Ron dished himself a few more potatoes and passed the bowl to David. "At first I was disappointed. I had big dreams. Maybe run a business or even become a lawyer. But it turns out, I didn't need college for any of that. I run a darn good business right here, and lawyering? Well, with just about every piece of land I've bought and business I've built here, there's legal work to do. It all worked out."

"Well, today's different, Dad. Everyone who can afford college should go to college. Even if it's just to grow up and learn how to live on your own," David chimed in. He felt a need to balance the conversation.

Ron started laughing, "Really? You believe that? You think a kid can only learn responsibility at college? I say you drop one kid right here into Orchard Canyon and drop another kid behind a desk in a dorm room and I can tell you which one will come out in four years more responsible."

Ron wanted to be clear, "Meghan, I do think you need to go to college, but understand that college is just more school. The real school happens outside this house, outside your house, outside the classroom. Take the advice from an old guy. Experience as much as you can outside of school. More than that even," Ron was looking right at Meghan who was looking right back at him for the first time. The two were so focused on each other that neither saw the disbelief on David's face.

David had to interject, "Dad, are you kidding me? You were the grand proponent of college when I was Meghan's age. Now you're not? I can't believe it. I just can't believe it. College was a given for me. There was no staying here or taking off a year to find myself. College was next. Done. Right after high school."

"I'm still a fan of college, but things were a lot different then, son. College was more affordable. I may dress like a farmer, but I'm really a businessman in work pants and boots. The return on the college investment was better when you were 17. If college today were a crop, I might leave the field barren. In some cases, it wouldn't pay to farm it."

"So you're saying Meghan should sit on the couch after she graduates high school until she figures out what she wants to do?" David asked with an edge to his voice. This was the *last* conversation he wanted to have tonight. Meghan already had voiced some crazy ideas about trying to get into the entertainment business, maybe work on a reality show or become a professional host, both of which required a lucky break more than a college degree. This discussion was not helping. Of all the awkward conversation scenarios that David played out in his head about dinner at Dad's, this was not one of them.

Meghan watched the ping pong match wondering if either of them cared what she thought. "I do want to go to college," she broke in. "But I also want to do something I love. I'm just not sure what that is. I know I like social media, I like keeping up with celebrities and fashion and stuff like that. I just don't know how that fits into anything other than 'stuff I like to do.' I mean are there any classes in school for that? Are there jobs?"

"Every one of those industries you mentioned, Meghan, need people to manage the money. That's why I say accounting, finance, those are safe bets. And you're an excellent math student," David said.

"But she might not want to be the bean counter. She might want to be the designer," Ron said, then interrupting himself and directing his attention to Meghan. "Meghan, you know what I mean? There's nothing wrong with either one—bean counter, designer—it just comes down to what you like. I don't know if you've had time to really figure that out yet, honey. But I can tell you one thing, if you follow what you love, you'll be happier in life."

"That's what I see with Mom!" Meghan said, the emotion of discovery showing in her voice. "She looks like she's having fun. I mean she has to 'count the beans' but she gets to do lots of other things like design websites and think up products. Actually she has someone working for her who does the counting, now that I think of it. That's Jason. Her job seems exciting." Meghan decided to try a Brussels sprout. "These are actually really good. I think I'll add them to my chicken fingers phase," she looked up and smiled at Ron. He smiled back knowing that they had a formed a tiny connection.

David didn't see it that way. He was convinced that Meghan was being brainwashed by both Susan and now his own father. David was in no position tonight to be the champion of taking the safe road. How safe was his stable career after all? Not very, at the moment. He resigned himself to finish the food on his plate and keep quiet. It was just a bad day. He'd get another job soon enough, probably making even more money, and then he would be a solid voice of reason with his daughter. His belief would be restored.

Let it go, he thought, then said, "Who's up for that walk?"

Chapter 5

With time spent on a walk through the orchard, business talk about the resort and improvements for next season, the dishes nearly cleared and everyone talked out, thankfully, David finally said, "Well, we'd better head out. Tomorrow's a work day." Meghan shot her dad a glance, not sure if he just forgot he had no work to go to or if he was just covering. "And it's getting late."

"Well, this has been perfect. Let's make it something we do more often. Can we? We don't get together as much as we should. And even though I have lots of friends here, there's nothing like family." Ron felt he had the right, this time, to play another tiny, little guilt card.

"I think that would be fun, Dad. I'd be up for it," Meghan said looking at Ron and seeing his eyes twinkle.

David felt ganged up on, "Well, we'll see. Meghan. You have a lot going on with school and dance, and ..." his voice trailed off as Ron and Meghan began planning next week's activities.

"There's a lot around this place you haven't seen yet, Meghan. It's full of surprises," Ron said while David grabbed their jackets.

"So you'll take me into the barn next time? I bet there's some really cool stuff in there," Meghan asked, her eyes full of an explorer's wonder.

"Oh there is and you bet I will. But dress for it, okay. Blue jeans, boots, dress warmer. It's getting colder up here. Not those tall shoes and that little jacket you have on today. You'll turn your ankle and freeze in a second. There might even be snow," Ron said looking head to toe at the budding fashionista.

"Got it. Jeans, boots, warmer jacket. Snow would be amazing!"

"Okay, good. We gotta go. Thanks for everything, Dad ..." David waved as he was heading for the door.

"Yeah, thanks for everything!" chimed in Meghan, but with sincerity. She looked over her shoulder at Ron and smiled.

"Bye, bye now. Drive carefully. I'll call you." Ron waved and as he did, his heart warmed. He thought, *That Meghan, she is a lovely child.* But concern crept into his thoughts. *David. Something's up with David.*

"Well, that was really fun," Meghan said as she closed the door to the car and grabbed her seat belt, strapping herself in.

"What was fun?" David asked, pausing for a moment from putting on his own seat belt to look at his daughter. He knew his daughter and could tell by the lilt in her voice that she didn't mean the trip to her grandfather's was fun.

"Ha! It was fun watching you and your dad go at it today, back and forth. It's nice to see I'm not the only one who doesn't agree with my parental unit sometimes," Meghan had to chuckle at catching her dad being more real, less dad-like, and more like a son.

David was not happy. He truly had felt like a child again the moment he sat in his old chair at the kitchen table, and at one point during the dinner, he came close to acting like one. *God, that house gets me every time,* he thought.

"We weren't 'going at it,' Meghan. People don't always agree, particularly people from different generations. Your grandfather has spent a lot of time, his whole life, in that canyon. He doesn't know how cutthroat the world is now. He doesn't know how important it is to have a college degree. He's persuasive, so don't confuse that with him knowing anything about what it takes to succeed in the 21st century." Meghan had to agree. Her grandfather did have a fun kind of energy around him that she hadn't really noticed before. She liked it, surprisingly, but her dad's comment made her question her grandfather's wisdom for a split second. And that's all it was. She shook it off.

Just then, in the early throes of what David felt could be a recovery, a reclamation of some parental ground, his phone rang through the car Bluetooth. He looked at Meghan. "It's your mother."

"Pick it up!" Meghan said. She wanted to tell her mom all about their day.

"Hey, Susan. How's it going?" David delivered his standard greeting. He hadn't talked to his ex-wife in a few weeks. She'd been traveling and he wasn't much for picking up the phone and calling.

"Great! How are you? Are you in the car?" Susan could tell from the hum of the motor in the background.

"Yesss ... Hi, Mom!" Meghan's spirits were clearly in a different place driving back to Scottsdale than they were a few hours earlier on the ride up. And she was far more buoyant than her dad.

"Hi, honey. So nice to hear your voice. What are you and your dad up to?"

"We were just at Dad's place for the day and an early dinner," David said matter-of-factly. "Heading home now." If the events of the day could have been left at that, David would have considered the trip a recovered success, but he knew better. This conversation was just beginning. Susan was inquisitive.

"Yeah, it was actually pretty fun, Mom. We're going to be coming back in a couple weeks when I'm at Dad's. I'm going to get to see the barn," Meghan pictured the barn as a treasure trove or at the very least a place with cute animals. She wasn't sure which, but would be prepared for both.

"Well, we're not sure about timing. We have to check schedules ..." David quickly interjected.

"You were at Ron's farm?" Susan's interruptive statement came out sounding a little too much like a question. Truth was, she was surprised the two had visited. *I hope nothing's wrong,* she thought. "How's your dad, David?" Susan continued, not waiting for David's typical blather about being too busy, yada,

yada, yada. She believed you make time for the things that are important to you. That's how she ran her life, and surprise! It worked.

Meghan continued, "He's fine. I found out I like ham and Brussels sprouts and that Dad and his dad don't agree on whether I should go to college or not. It was fun to watch. Dad was this close to ..." she held her thumb and forefinger about a quarter-inch apart, "this close to flinging a mini-cabbage at him."

"She's talking about the Brussels sprouts and I was not that close to flinging anything," he said, making the same gesture. "You're really making more of this than it was, Meghan."

"Well, I'm not sure whose side I'm taking, or maybe it's my own side," said Susan. "I do think college is important, but it's what you do while you're there—outside of the classroom—that matters, too. Maybe more. Oh and find something you love. That makes all the difference. But we've talked about that before, haven't we, honey?"

David mouthed silently to Meghan, "You've talked about this?" Meghan just raised her brows and cocked her head. David was not about to enter the ring for round two.

"You asked how Dad is, Susan. He's good. As you can tell, he's as opinionated as ever," David said, unable to help himself. Meghan just smiled and shook her head.

"Well, my guess is, I'd favor his opinion on this topic. College for me was fine, but it wasn't everything. And it certainly didn't guarantee me getting to bank vice president, that's for sure. And the irony? I've learned more about finance since starting the business than I ever did in college or even at the bank. And loving every minute of it!"

David's silence was deafening.

Realizing she had probably said too much, Susan shifted gears., "Hey, I won't keep you. You're probably tired and want to get back to town. David, I was going to ask you, but since I have you both on the phone at once, I was thinking about the winter school break. Meghan, you seemed to enjoy working at the company over the summer, would you want to work a few days a week downtown during your break?"

Susan had built the company she started right after the birth of Meghan into a $15-million dollar online powerhouse, and growing. After her maternity leave, she just couldn't bring herself to part with her newborn baby, and the thought of going back to her dead-end job at the bank was throwing her into a legitimate depression. She just couldn't do it. But money was tight, too tight.

Chapter 5

Susan, in between nursing and napping and diaper-changing, started a website that allowed budding clothing designers to set up a storefront and launch their lines. It proved to be a viable way for designers to build a following and get noticed. It started small and in the first few months she made hardly anything, maybe $50. But little by little, the site began generating more interest. Now, based in Phoenix, it had been called the YouTube of fashion design, launching almost as many talented designers as YouTube has launched performing artists.

Meghan smiled and, before David could make up an excuse or say, "We'll have to see," she blurted, "That'd be awesome! I'd love that!"

"Okay with you, David? It wouldn't be too much time, but it's a good learning experience for Meghan and doesn't hurt on a resume, either." Susan knew David well. She knew she would have to plead her case a bit. The resume thing was hard to refute in David's world. Susan knew she had him.

"No, that's fine. That'd be great. Meghan, if it's something you want to do."

"It is, it is!" Meghan said without hesitation and gesturing little mini-claps with her hands. She liked the people and the energy at Susan's company.

Susan started to laugh, "David, I can always tell when you're not on board. You always start with 'No,' and say something like 'that's fine.' Like you're trying to convince yourself. Meghan, he'll get used to it. Can't wait for you to be part of the team again. Just a couple weeks from now! Okay, I'll let you both go. Meghan, you're staying with your dad tonight, right? I'll see you after school tomorrow. So long!"

David and Meghan confirmed the plans and said, "Bye" in unison. Meghan settled into her seat and felt that this day turned out way better than she had expected. David locked his hands on the wheel and thought, *Just 60 more miles and this day will be over.*

But what about tomorrow? *That's going to be weird*, David's mind went to the worst. His daughter was going to get up and have somewhere to go. It was a school day. She had people to see, responsibilities. And what would he have? He should probably go to the unemployment office, but that's hardly something to look forward to. Actually it's even more demoralizing than staying home while the world commutes. Thank God for online filing. Okay, so he has that task, but what else? He was starting to get that feeling in the pit of his stomach. It was a blend of loneliness, loss, fear, embarrassment, and anger. He hadn't felt it in several years, not since the last time he was out of work. But like emotions triggered from a sad song, the thought of 7:00 am sank his heart. He said nothing the rest of the ride back to Phoenix and the Valley of the Sun.

CHAPTER 6

That night when David and Meghan got home, they each went about their business. Home life became home life once again. The trip to Disneyland, a.k.a. Orchard Canyon, was over. Meghan donned her PowerBeats and quickly selected a playlist as her musical accompaniment to checking her Instagram and gathering up her stuff for school tomorrow. She snapped a picture of her "pile of craziness," and posted it. Her friends entered into the dialog about how much homework is too much homework based on that one photo of her desk strewn with papers, her laptop, and books that represented her senior project in progress.

She was in the midst of researching what life was like in the '40s and trying her best to narrow down the subject to something that wouldn't be boring. Of course her dad wanted her to write about something to do with money. Like how America financed World War II with war bonds. That was one of his suggestions. *Yeah, no way. That's boring.* What she really wanted to write about was fashion in the '40s but thought her teacher may feel the subject was not serious enough for a senior capstone project. Even though Meghan knew she'd love the subject, she didn't want to forfeit an A before she typed in a single word.

So between online gripes and laughs, OMGs, and WTFs, Meghan continued to get organized and contemplate both her day and anything that caught her eye online. Research on the subject of the '40s was like following a bunny trail that somehow always led to Kim Kardashian. Meghan clicked on a picture of Kim wearing what looked like a yellow plastic bodysuit and posted, "Who designs this stuff? In a second, one of her friends posted, "WHO ELSE would wear it!!? :-b." And so the evening went with at least 20 of Meghan's closest friends chiming in on posts as each followed their own online bunny trails.

David's evening was very different from Meghan's. With no diversions left, David was beginning to sink into a real funk. Monday morning loomed; it was just 10 hours away. It loomed like a monster in his mind now. He was alone. He had nowhere to go. He felt unneeded and without purpose.

Why am I taking this so hard, David asked himself. *God knows this is not the first time I've lost my job. Get a grip!* But this time his layoff was different. He was older and he was not even close to where he thought he'd be at this age. Who was he kidding? There was a time during the dot-com boom of the late '90s when he thought he and Susan would be able to retire at 40. Now here he was, in debt, paying off the very couch he was sitting on and practically everything else in the room, with a pitiful, dwindling bank account. He couldn't help but think as a banker, *I have officially become a bad risk.*

It was more than that. It was his father. It was Susan. The conversations tonight had shaken him. David didn't want to admit it but he couldn't help but wonder if, somehow, while he was crunching numbers and taking care of other people's businesses, the world had changed. Had he become one of those people who, when beginning his career, he had looked at and said under his breath, "Get with the times, old man! Put away the adding machine and use Lotus 1-2-3!" Was he living in the past, basing his future on beliefs that were no longer true? Or maybe not as certain as they used to be.

The thought of all this rattled his foundation. It was a lot like how he felt when Iraq invaded Kuwait and America entered the first Gulf War—Operation

Desert Storm. Like so many people David's age, he was used to Middle East strife. But America planning to fly planes and drop bombs rocked his illusion of stability and safety in the world. He hadn't experienced war until then. Was his belief in the security of the path—go to college, get a job—an illusion? Was the security of his life an illusion? Had the way to get somewhere, be somebody, get rich changed so much that his beliefs had run their course? These were questions he didn't want to know the answers to, and he certainly didn't want to go there tonight. "Not tonight," David unconsciously said out loud.

Meghan happened to walk in the living room at precisely that moment. "Not tonight, what?"

"What?" David asked, looking like he had been snatched from some other world and plopped into reality again.

"You said 'Not tonight,' and I just wondered ..."

"Oh, it was nothing, I don't even know ..."

"Okay." Meghan let it drop. Parents can just be so weird. She began walking to the kitchen and then stopped, "You know, I was thinking about going back to the farm next weekend and getting that barn tour. I just keep imagining it full of all kinds of cool stuff. I can drive up myself. Mom won't mind." And having learned well from her mother how to get her dad's buy in by creating a reason that he can't refute, "Plus, I'm working on researching my topic for my senior class project. I think my answer might just be in that barn. It has to be full of old relics that could be great inspiration. I mean your dad lived through the time period in America that we are studying. I really want my project to focus on history and apply it to today somehow."

David, still not quite out of his own head, replied simply, "That's fine, Meghan."

"So I can go?" Meghan was a little surprised. This was way too easy. *I must be getting good at this,* she thought! That's step one.

Meghan sped off into her room and pulled out the small piece of paper her grandfather had handed her before she left. On it was a gmail address, his own, with two words, "Email me!" Looking at it in her hand, she had to chuckle. He had an ancient TV, faucets that came out of the wall *and* a Google account. That struck her as a little funny since her own dad didn't even have a Google account.

> *Hi. Thanks for today. I was wondering if I could come see the barn next Saturday. I'd have to make sure my mom is fine with it, but is that OK with you?*
> *~ Meghan*

Chapter 6

Ron always checked his email in the morning, so Meghan would have to wait for a response. In the meantime, she got back to looking at topics for her paper. Maybe she would do a project about college then and now. That would be timely. She looked up how much it costs to go to UCLA now and found it costs around $60,000 per year for out-of-state tuition. *Wow, that's a lot*, she thought. *What about in 1940; how much did it cost then per year?*

She did a quick search and found out that tuition was free for California residents in 1956, the closest date she could find, and $300 a year for non-residents. She also found that $300 in 1956 was the same as $2,700 in today's money. Something didn't add up. It seemed college costs had gone crazy. No wonder her grandfather questioned whether college was a good deal or not. She looked closer and found that tuition started to really escalate in the 2000s and wondered why.

After her quick study, she decided against this topic. *It's too depressing.* No wonder so many of her friends' older brothers and sisters had student loans they whined about. And no wonder all those pop-up ads about paying off your student loans were everywhere online. One of them said the average college student graduates with about $40,000 in student loans. Some of the ads posted even higher numbers. *Good thing I won't need to take out loans.* She breathed a sigh of relief.

Then she thought of her mom's company and wondered how easy it was in the '40s to start a business. She loved that aspect of her mother's career, that one day she just stopped doing one thing and started something else, literally from nothing. That intrigued her. *Did people do that back then?* she wondered.

David got up from the couch and shook his shoulders. It was his attempt to snap himself back into reality and his place of stability. But that place wasn't there. "Meghan," he called, "I think I'm going to go read in the den. If you need anything that's where I'll be."

Meghan didn't hear any of that, she had her PowerBeats on listening to her favorite YouTuber while she dreamed of what it must have been like to start a business in 1948. *I think that's what my paper will be about. What it was like back then to work and go into business in America.*

Chapter 7

Chapter 7

Ron, who never left a pile of dirty dishes in the sink for any length of time, was drying the last of the plates and putting them on the open shelves next to the sink. His mind however was reliving the day and the connection he felt he made with Meghan. He wondered how long it would take her to reach out to him, if ever.

When the last plate was neatly on the shelf and the dish towel hung to dry, Ron turned the lights off in the kitchen and went into the living room to see what was happening in the world. CNN was his favorite channel. The news of the day typically included updates on the latest political scandal, news about Syria or some other foreign land, commentary on the U.S. economy and when Ron walked in, coincidentally, the future of banking. "Some experts are predicting," said the talking head on TV, "that 50 percent of the retail banks as we know them will be gone in 10 years. Technology is replacing the need for people in branches." Ron heard that snippet and wondered how that might affect David. Ron didn't completely understand the scope of David's work but he couldn't help but think this signaled bad news. Right now, however, all he could think of was Meghan and David, how much he enjoyed seeing them and ... He suddenly got the urge to check his email.

"Well, by gosh, an email from Meghan, already!" Ron was ecstatic. As much as their visit was the highpoint of the day, this was the icing on the cake. He decided he would play it cool and not look overly eager. "I'll email her when I get up to do the morning chores," he decided. "She'll have her 'yes' answer by the time she wakes up."

The other thing Ron kept revisiting during the evening was the whole conversation about career, about choosing something for the money versus choosing something because of the experience, the enjoyment. He was surprised to learn that David really seemed to believe the money came first. "You go for the money and that takes care of the rest."

Ron was trying to figure out where David got that notion. *It had to be working for all those dang banks,* he thought. There are a lot of people in that boat. Ron certainly sees and hears it from his friends. Being trapped on the corporate ladder, and hand-cuffed financially through the promise of annual bonuses and the realities of excessive family spending. They just live life to get through the workday, eager for the weekend. Ron has friends whose kids are living that way. *It's probably a lot more common than I realize.*

Ron knew about happiness and fulfillment. He credited living a full 82 years and counting, to living happy. That's the best medicine. In life, there's no replacement for loving what you do and how you spend your days. He's been the "CEO" of Orchard Canyon for over 50 years, including the orchards, the resort, the restaurant, the cider business, all of it. And he has had no regrets for his lot in life. In fact, even though Ron had wanted to go to college when he was a restless teenager, he had learned all the principles of operating a complex business on the farm. College, he realized years ago, is not the only pathway to education.

As Ron mentioned to David and Meghan, this place in the canyon has been his college. Economics, marketing, finance, sales, real estate, distribution, all of it he learned at Orchard Canyon University. In fact, he learned about commodities, about retail, margins, working with grocers, product quality, construction, customer service and so much more.

One of the bigger lessons was supply and demand. Ron had good years when the trees produced a lot of apples and other years when the harvest was weak. During those lean years, the work went from harvesting to sourcing the apples for cider and still making a profit. Being a fruit grower is a tough business along with tough work. Good thing he loved it. Otherwise, he never would have lasted so long. It's just too non-stop, too tiring, too unpredictable. But that's the point, you don't mind the ups and downs if you love what you're doing.

Did David have that? Ron thought about those times when David would talk about work, which were rare. Come to think of it, Ron couldn't remember a single work conversation where David had any fire in his voice or a posture of excitement in his body language. It was like he was going through the motions, often sighing through his words. *But he sure had a lot of nice things in that big house of his,* Ron thought. *Even with the money he was making, the stuff never seemed like enough, though.* Ron paused on that thought and again wondered what was up with David.

Those thoughts weighed heavy on Ron's heart as he watched a little more news then turned in for the night. No father wants to see his son unhappy. And clearly David is—Ron could feel it—even with the front David tried to put on today. Ron began thinking about the old days, 45 years ago. His heart leapt at the number 45 after he thought it. Has it really been that long? It was the midst of the Vietnam War and tensions were high in America. Even within those volatile times, there were good times too. Lots of them. He remembered one in particular:

"I didn't miss it, did I?" a young David yelled from the front door as he dropped his Stingray bike on the front porch and his text books on the table just inside the door.

"No you're in time. They're still at T-minus 10 minutes, 10 seconds. Hurry, get yourself in here." Ron called. He was so glad David had made it home. He wanted to watch the Apollo launch with his whole family.

"David, here, sit down." David's mom pointed to the couch and moved the morning newspaper out of the way to make room. "I'll get us some Tang. David, you have to be hot."

"I am, Mom. I rode as fast as I could. Watching the replay just isn't the same thing as seeing the actual launch."

"T-minus eight minutes," Walter Cronkite interrupted. "Eight minutes to launch." Ron got up to see if he could get the picture a little clearer by adjusting the antenna on the top of their TV set.

"That looks better; let's see if it stays," Ron said knowing how finicky TV reception could be.

David got comfortable sitting cross-legged on the couch with his elbows on his knees and eyes glued to the TV set as if he wanted to climb into it. Ever since the very first Apollo launch that he could remember, David had wanted to be an astronaut. He and countless other young boys of that era. To ride in a rocket, orbit the moon, wear a space suit, and splash down in some foreign ocean. How cool was that! Plus the training was like riding the rides at the amusement park all day long. David was fascinated by that "spinning thing," as he called it, that simulated the super high g-forces the astronauts would have to withstand at take-off and reentry.

"Thanks, Mom," David said as he took the glass of Tang off the tray barely looking away from the TV set. It was the same drink the astronauts were drinking on board the spacecraft!

"T-minus three minutes," David, his parents, and Mr. Cronkite said almost in unison.

"Dad, that's going to be me when I grow up. Hey, Mom, you'll get to go to Florida to watch. I bet they let families come and watch the launch,"

David said, not just excited for this launch, but for his future. His eyes were wide, glued to the screen and his heartbeat was escalating with every tick of the countdown clock. He guzzled half the Tang and wiped his mouth on his arm.

"I can barely stand it. I don't know what I'll do when you're going into space, David. I'll be a nervous wreck," his mother said. David was mesmerized. He barely heard his mother's words.

"Well, study hard, son. Those men are the brightest and the best. You have to get good grades in school, then go to college and get good grades there too. You'll do it. I know you will," said Ron.

Everyone's eyes were glued to the TV now. "Ten, nine, eight, seven, six, five, four, three, two, one, zero ... We have lift off. Apollo 11 is now heading into space as the first manned spacecraft mission to the moon."

What Ron didn't know was that between that momentous and memorable launch, and when Captain Eugene Cernan, on December 17, 1972, became the last man on the moon, David's dream of rocketing into space turned into the countless, mundane hours of class time and homework in the public schools of the 70s. Teachers teaching. Students dozing, messing around, and cramming for quizzes and tests. Panicking and, in David's case, stressing over the possibility of anything less than an A. Everyone had to fit into the mold and luckily that mold was made for David.

Guidance counselors would base their advice on classroom behavior, grades, and the standardized tests of the day, as if everyone learned and tested exactly the same. Kids who were likely brilliant, but bored and disruptive—the future entrepreneurs who didn't fit into the mold—got low grades and were often deemed not college material. The school would track them into curriculum programs so they could land trade jobs their senior year, rather than college acceptance letters.

David was not one of those. He had become the high-strung perfect student who felt like a failure if he didn't get an A. Even in gym class. His 10th grade guidance counselor, Mrs. Jenkins, told him he had quite an aptitude for numbers. *That has to be good for the space program*, David excitedly thought. He was sure the next words out of the Mrs. Jenkins' mouth would be, "David, you are destined for engineering, aeronautics, or even NASA."

But instead she said, "David, you keep up this good work and you'll make a fine banker. There are always plenty of jobs for bankers. Everyone puts their money in a bank and that means banks need people like you to keep track of it."

"I was thinking about maybe going to work with NASA, you know, the space program. Kinda like, be an astronaut one day," David was a little embarrassed to share his dream so openly with a stranger. Mrs. Jenkins and he had never said a word to each other before this session. But that's how a lot of counseling was and maybe still is.

"An astronaut? Why would you want to do that? Those men are heroes, for sure, but you are looking at a long shot there, David," she said shaking her head. "Do you know how many kids your age want to be astronauts? The likelihood of making it is very small. What would you fall back on? That's a fun dream for a child, but David, you're growing up. Banking, that's a career, a good one for a smart young man like you. I gathered up some college brochures here that have very good accounting degree programs. I think you should take them home and show them to your parents. I'll be setting up a guidance session with them later in the year. You have time to think about your future. But do think about it realistically, David."

That was David's cue to get up and leave. "Thank you, Mrs. Jenkins."

Chapter 7

"You're welcome, David. You have a very bright future."

And that was it. David felt foolish leaving Mrs. Jenkins' office, still clinging to his childhood dreams of space travel. The whole notion started to sound babyish to him. *She's right, I'd have nothing to fall back on. Did she expect me to fail?*, he wondered.

Accounting. What exactly is accounting? He felt disappointed, empty and lost. So much of his whole life had been spent looking at the stars, imagining himself among them. *Kid stuff*, he thought. When he got home, he dropped his books and instead of his normal glass of Tang, he poured himself a glass of ice tea. He never drank a glass of Tang again.

That's the truth that Ron never knew. Does anyone really know how children lose their dreams? This is certainly one way. Adults and teachers in particular are influential. A little bit of encouragement can go a long way. But in David's case, as was the case with so many students then and maybe even now, education was about making sure standardized test scores were kept high. It wasn't about truly getting to know the students, their aspirations, and guiding them toward a fulfilling life. Meghan certainly wasn't getting that kind of guidance. She was just as in the dark about her talents and how they could be applied in the real world as David was decades before. And, she's just as clueless about the jobs the world has to offer as David was.

Ron sat in his living room that night and wondered what did happen to David and his dream to go to the moon. It seemed to have just fallen away. One day he was gazing at the stars and the next day he didn't care. Or maybe he did and something happened. Maybe David's career wasn't the one he really wanted. He seemed so good at it, how could he not love it? Then he remembered that David did well at everything, even things he didn't really like doing. That's when it hit him. Maybe David was unhappy at his job.

Chapter 8

CHAPTER 8

Ron guessed right. Maybe David's dream got crushed. From Mrs. Jenkins forward, he took the safe bet, the well-beaten path, and he has been taking it ever since that moment in tenth grade. He became an astronaut-turned-banker, before he ever made it to flight school. He was still in that g-force "spinning thing" trying to endure high school and all that came with it. The teachers, the mundane classes, the awkwardness of the age.

He became a master test taker. Multiple choice was his grand forte. His prowess was nearly zen-like. And he was aptly rewarded for it. A's. Always A's. His parents were so proud. When it came to applying to colleges, David could have gone anywhere, but knowing his dad needed him at Orchard Canyon fairly often, he elected to stay closer to home and go to ASU. It was a good school with a good accounting program and it was safe. Some of the kids he graduated with would be going there too. It would be like moving his high school clan south from Sedona to Tempe. That was comforting and safe. The thought of showing up at a school and knowing absolutely no one was terrifying.

Now as David lay in his own bed, he was thinking about just how "safe" his safe bet really was. Tomorrow was the first day of the rest of his life, trouble was, he didn't have much of a life at the moment. He felt he was now at that college where he knew no one. It was called World U.

Time had moved on. He was starting to think that the banking world he was part of—no, *is* part of—moves at the pace of a snail. That's the environment he has been living in for his entire career and he liked it. Change? Who wants change? Change just creates chaos. It makes you anxious. Who needs that? So David resisted it.

Early in his career, banking seemed so static, everything always the same. What David didn't see was that banking was one of the first things to begin transforming in the digital age. Not because the industry wanted to change, but because customers demanded the automation convenience. ATM machines began affecting the face of banking decades ago. The teller became a machine with buttons and slots. People used to think that technology would only affect blue collar factory workers through automation. Technology has always affected everyone, and it continues to affect everyone. The banking industry was flying forward much faster than it seemed in the moment. And David not only missed it, he avoided seeing it.

Thinking back, he even had two opportunities to move into areas of banking that are far more secure today. When David got his first banking job, he was heavily recruited by the Information Systems team who wanted his excellent performance record and attention to detail. That would have tracked him away from accounting and into technology. He didn't take it. Didn't want to risk his banking future. The computer room seemed like a dark recess away from the bright light of high-power finance. Being in finance, that's where the glory and the recognition lived. That's where David thought he had the best shot at the top floor and a corner office. And probably so, but the decision came with risks.

Another opportunity came later. He was offered the controller position with a small start-up company that later became Infusionsoft, a true Arizona technology success story. He was even offered stock options that were worth nothing at the time. Had he taken this opportunity, he would have been employee number four at an $80 million company that he owned a part of.

Even, years later when everyone else was diving headlong into the Internet age and the social networking culture, David kept himself an outcast. He hadn't embraced any of that stuff and thought it was a massive waste of time. Who has time to create and manage a LinkedIn account? What is the purpose other than to take up a lot of time he didn't have? *I don't care who has made a job change or who got a promotion. I don't want to join the Arizona CFO Group or my ASU Alumni Group and answer a bunch of people's business or money questions for free.*

That was how David saw social media. But it was also his outlook on life. He was on his way somewhere and didn't have time for relationships. Didn't want to let people in too far. "They just disappoint you," he would tell Susan the few times he got close to colleagues.

He looked down on his own daughter for how much time she spent in front of one glowing screen or another. Okay, so maybe her behavior is excessive, but he was beginning to think just maybe his own loner behavior was too. And perhaps not very smart. He began listing in his head the number of people in his network. It was becoming frighteningly clear that the people he could call friends or even associates were very few. And the people he did know were in the same predicament he was.

He dozed off striving to add to the mental list of who he was going to call in the morning to start once again—how many times was this going to happen?—his job search. He fell asleep fast because he stalled out at about five names and simply couldn't think of any more. The day had taken its toll on him.

In his own dreams that night, he saw himself wandering through a busy city street, people everywhere, bumping into him. Faces everywhere, he saw them, but he knew none of them. They were all going somewhere and he wasn't. He was just slowly walking upstream, being pushed and shoved, his back to the horizon in a sea of people all heading toward their futures. The moonless sky was starless too.

Chapter 9

Chapter 9

"Dad! Where's my purse? I put it on the counter last night and you cleaned off the counter, so where did you put it?" That was David's alarm clock at 7:11 exactly. "Have you seen it? You must have seen it." Meghan was not running late, she was just excited for her day. She awoke to an email from her grandfather saying he was more than happy to show her the barn. She told him she'd be there early on Sunday.

"It's in the media room, and I didn't move it. That's where you put it." Still groggy, David pulled himself out of bed and sardonically thought to himself, *Happy Monday. Happy life.* He walked into the kitchen and saw that Meghan had retrieved her purse and was stocking it with the day's lip gloss selections.

"My ride will be here in a few minutes, and I'll call you later today. I texted Mom this morning about going back to Orchard Canyon on Sunday. So she's picking me up after school so we can go shopping. I want to get some warmer clothes since we're going to be in the barn and everything. You should come with me Sunday!"

"You're going to the farm next weekend?" David was half asleep, and he completely ignored the invitation. The last thing he knew he'd want to hear next Sunday was the loaded question from his father, "Hi David, how was your week?"

"Daaad," Meghan said, dragging out the word like only an annoyed teenager can do, "I told you last night. We're going to explore the barn. I think I might get inspiration for my senior project." Meghan pushed the same irrefutable argument in David's sheet-creased face that she did the night before.

David really didn't remember talking about this the night before, but he wasn't in a position to argue. And besides, it was Susan's weekend with Meghan. "Okay. That's fine. If your mom says it's okay. But I hope you don't plan on staying late. I don't want you driving that distance in the dark."

"Yay! Then maybe you'll come with me! So I don't have to drive in the dark." She smiled, sweetly kissed her dad, waved bye and was out the door.

School couldn't end fast enough. Meghan was antsy all day long to talk to her mom about her trip to the farm and to get some cool boots to wear. She also was imagining her time there. She was dying to know what was awaiting her in that old barn. In fifth period study hall, she caught herself daydreaming about what life must have been like in the '40s—that's the period her class is studying in history class—the war, industrialization, the prolonged economic struggles, and also the opulence of the times. She was enamored.

One more period to go and it's history, she thought. So she could dash right out of her class and go shopping, Meghan went to her locker after study hall and grabbed her things and brought them with her to her last class.

Meghan was doodling in her notebook, listening as her teacher went on about The Great Depression. "When the stock market crashed in 1929, it set the nation into a panic. People everywhere ran to the banks frantically trying to get their money out of their accounts. Some banks locked their doors, causing even more panic. That sent the nation into a terrible economic time where lots of people found themselves in soup lines. The government had programs to provide food to people who were nearly destitute ..."

Her grandfather, too, spent an hour or so that day daydreaming and preparing what he might want to show her in the old barn. *Even though I have my own idea of what she might like to see, I have to make it feel like discovery to her*, he thought. Ron wasn't being manipulative. He simply knew how to make things fun.

Ron hadn't been through that part of the barn in years. The tractors, the tools, the cider press his orchard managers used daily. But in the deep recesses of the barn's far corners, living amongst the dust, were relics from the past that he hadn't seen in 40 years. Many were his and his wife's. But some were his parents' possessions that no one ever went through when they both passed on.

Ron climbed over a few rusty rolls of fence wire and spotted the corner of what looked like an old wooden apple crate. *An apple crate! We can always use one more of those,* Ron said to himself. He began lifting the old tractor parts that had all but buried the crate. A strong 82-year-old, he had no trouble dragging an old axel and tie-rod out of the way. Under it Ron spotted a few bona fide vintage tractor seats and a heap of random engine parts both in the crate and overflowing it. *This is a lot of work just to salvage an apple crate, but what the heck*, Ron thought as he methodically began removing the tractor parts and placing them on the shelves against the far wall. He wasn't planning on straightening up the barn today, but so it went until he stumbled upon a real find. "By gosh, is that a jar? Full of coins?"

Judging by the age of the crate and how old the tractor parts were on top of the jar, the coins inside could easily be a hundred years old! They were fully concealed, completely out of sight, which made Ron wonder if his parents or grandparents had stashed them for a rainy day and then forgot about them. Finally able to grab the rust-hinged glass lid—it looked like an old canning jar—Ron pulled the jar from the crate. Through the cloudy glass, he could make out dimes, nickels, pennies, quarters, maybe even some silver dollars.

He opened the jar and poured a few coins into his hand. He could barely make out the dates. "Looks like a 1929 nickel," he said to an audience of no one. "Here's 1928, 1932, 1940, 1937." He could see the currency was from a time period when silver coins were actually silver and a dime was worth a dime's worth of silver. From 1920 to 1964 coins were made of mostly silver. Given the price of silver today, that 25-cent coin that Ron was holding is worth about $3.50 based on its silver content. "Today, quarters feel like tin compared to this," he said forgetting how heavy change once felt in his pocket. "I guess 25 cents doesn't even pay for much of a coin these days. With inflation, 25 cents doesn't pay much of anything." He put the coins back in the jar and stashed them back in the apple crate so Meghan could rediscover them when she arrived. *I'll just cover them up with one of these tractor seats. That should do it,* Ron said to himself. Ron now had one good discovery for Meghan if all else failed to catch her eye.

As Ron walked back to his house, those coins really got him thinking about these times we live in and how much the world had changed. He never liked being that guy who would say, "I remember when a loaf of bread cost 10 cents." But he *could* remember when a loaf of bread cost 10 cents. Money was real money when it was backed by gold. There was only so much of it and when a dollar traded hands a dollar's worth of gold traded hands. Not anymore. Money is just paper, not backed by anything. More and more he was grateful to have the farm in a beautiful canyon on real estate that he could see, feel, smell, and walk on. Real estate that had real value, that couldn't be diluted on a whim and that keeps pace with inflation. He felt a sense of comfort and pride knowing that as long as he owned the farm, the orchard, and the resort, along with the commerce it generated, he would never have to worry about money.

He hadn't always felt so carefree. He had some some bad timing in his life, just like everyone else, when it came to money and investments. He had to make some unavoidable improvements to the main house way back in the '70s which he planned to pay for in cash. All that was fine until Mother Nature decided to completely destroy the apple crop that year. Not enough rain, then too much rain at exactly the wrong times. His cash flow became dangerously low. So low he had to take out a bank loan to cover the construction costs. Trouble was the loans during that time were 14 percent compared to the low single-digit loans available now. He literally was paying 14 cents for every dollar he borrowed. And the rates often went higher. Ron recalled those years well. He even made due with his old truck way longer than he wanted to. No one was buying cars at 20 percent interest.

He also had invested some money in the stock market at the time. He thought he'd make a return on his money. Within an 18-month period, the market lost 40 percent of its value and people were afraid to go near Wall Street. So the market stagnated for almost a decade. The Great Inflation they now call it. Thankfully, Ron rebounded his cash flow the following year with a good crop. His expenses, like fuel for example, were inflated, which meant he had to inflate the price of everything he produced. Still, through smart management, he was able to keep his market steady and prices affordable to the community.

Those were tough times but not as tough as they were for many people. He had a business that kept pace with inflation. He didn't have to worry about losing a job and then finding another one. He didn't have to worry about his pay not increasing at the rate the food at the grocery store was going up. He never really felt squeezed like so many. Again, he wanted to give thanks for this little canyon.

CHAPTER 10

While Meghan was off to school and watching the clock on the wall all day, daydreaming about her trip to the farm and her big find in the barn, David was figuring out what to do with his day. Thinking about his life was just too much. It had been five days and no bites on any job postings he had responded to. *I'll get through today and thank God it's Friday*, he thought. *First a cup of coffee.* While the coffee brewed he pulled out his phone and began looking through his contacts. He wasn't looking forward to it, but he knew he needed to make some calls to the five people on his list and likely others. He had hoped he wouldn't need to let anyone know he was unemployed. That a job would come up.

God, Roger Evans. I wonder what he's up to? I haven't talked to him in years. Wonder where he is, what he's doing? Truth was, David hadn't talked to anyone in years. He spent his days at work talking with whoever was near him at that moment. Whoever he needed right then. Trouble was, they were all either out of work too, or still at his old company. And in reality, they weren't really friends; acquaintances of proximity, more like.

He poured his cup and took it into his office. The first thing he did was fire up his computer to see how you go about filing for unemployment these days. He couldn't bring himself to do it earlier in the week. He was hopeful that a job would appear. Waiting for the search page to load, David looked to his right at the notification on his screen. *Ugh, the mortgage is due next week.* He opened a second window to check his bank accounts and instantly got a knot in the pit of his stomach. His three months' severance wasn't going to go very far. He owed $8,478 on his mortgage every month and, clicking on his credit cards to check the balances owed, he did some quick math and gasped, "How did these card balances get run up to $32,550?"

David was always good with other people's money but a relative disaster with his own. He wanted what he wanted and he'd buy it. Susan was the same way. And so was Meghan. It's how she was raised, and no one taught her otherwise. School certainly didn't. Why is that? Wouldn't it be a good idea to teach people about money when they are kids?

The furniture in the house, the cars, the boat—nearly everything in David and Meghan's life—was financed. Even the boots she got to explore the barn wouldn't really be hers. And of course those "assets"—that's what the bank where David had worked called the car and the boat—lost half their value the moment he signed for delivery. Not quite good investments. *Let's be honest. It's all the toys. That's how this balance got so high. Buying stuff and taking care of the stuff we bought. The stuff I bought.* David was starting to feel really bad. *How am I going to find a job to pay for all this?*

Distracted once more, David began scrolling through his contacts. *No real friends,* he thought. *Well, enough stalling; let me make that first call.* Punching the numbers in on his cell, a short delay, and the phone began ringing. "Good morning. I'm calling for Randy Watson. Is he in yet?"

"You're calling for Randy ...?" the voice on the other end trailed off. David had called Randy's office; he didn't feel he knew him well enough—or at all—to call his cell.

"Watson, Randy Watson," David remembered and quickly said.

"I'm sorry, we don't have a Randy Watson here. Can I connect you with someone else? What is it regarding?"

"No, that's okay. It's nothing. I'll try him at another number." David wanted to get off the line as quickly as he could. Humiliating. Humiliated. That's how he felt. *Maybe I should take a break,* David said to himself. *I wonder what's happening on the news...*

David got up and turned on CNN. He felt lower still. The world was going on, it was happening and he wasn't invited. Business was being transacted, stocks going up and going down, experts commenting on the economic impact of world events. It made him sick. *All these people are ahead of me. Damn, that guy looks young. He can't be more than 40.* His thoughts were not helping his state of mind. Others were achieving and right now he wasn't.

One talking head blurted out, "We are a debtor nation, don't you agree?" directing his leading question to a group of four wealth experts. The scrolling text at the bottom of the screen read The State of America – Few Ready for Retirement. The "expert's" response cut right to the chase: "The problem is we are a nation of consumers. We produce little and consume a lot. That goes for a lot of households. They spend more than they make."

The host continued, "Well, I'd like to share a statistic on that. Actually less than 62 percent of people have $1,000 in savings. That means almost half the nation is not at all prepared for any kind of outlier event. Like an illness, a major home repair, or the loss of a job."

He continued, "And job loss is real. In fact, right now even with our unemployment rather low, many people still find themselves out of work. Particularly in certain sectors of our economy like manufacturing. There continues to be a lot of job loss there. And of course in any sector that is consolidating."

Like banking. David finished the comment right in his own living room. How had he gotten himself into this situation?

Just as he thought it, the third talking head answered his question: "So much of this failure to save money stems from excessive credit card debt. People just are swimming in credit card bills and it's impossible to get ahead with interest rates at 24 percent and higher on card debt."

David could relate. He was barely afloat in his debtor-nation life. He had three months' severance and no money of any real amount in the bank. He needed to do something. Just then the moderator said, "So what do these unfortunate indebted people do? How do they get back on track?" *Nice label—unfortunate indebted people.*

David's ears perked up. They were talking directly to him, and he was curious. "Well, here are the top five ways to pave your way to more financial security. First, cut up your credit cards. Don't use them!" the expert blurted out. "Budget what you can spend each week. If you can't afford that fancy latte, skip it and have cup of coffee in the office break room."

"Another idea is to pay yourself first, even if you have debt, pay yourself that ten dollars you save on those two lattes every week! Even ten dollars is a start. That's $40 dollars a month, or $480 a year. That's almost a 50 percent increase in savings for those poor people who have only $1,000 in savings." David was feeling sicker by the minute because this was the same old advice and, while good for some people, $480 a year wasn't going to put a dent in his debt. He turned the television off.

Chapter 11

"Meghan! Long time no see! I'm just kidding," Ron greeted his granddaughter with a big smile and a hug that was not yet fully reciprocated. Meghan wasn't use to those kinds of greetings, except from her mom and dad. "C'mon in. Is your dad with you?" The door closed behind her.

"Hi. No, dad didn't come along. This is going to be cool. I can't wait to see the barn. I've been imagining all the hidden treasures in there," she had waited long enough she felt. "When can we go out and see it?"

"Well, right now, if that's what you want to do. I see you followed my advice and wore your barn clothes." Meghan smiled. Her new graphic tee, designer skinny jeans, and $400 Frye boots were as close to "barn clothes" as she could find and was willing to buy. Style still mattered.

Chapter 11

They walked out the back door and Meghan looked to the west. There it was. The treasure barn. As they walked across the back garden area toward the tractor shed, she shared how she had to come up with a really good senior project. "I'm just stuck on what my topic should be. I wanted it to be about fashion, but I'm afraid my teacher will think that's a worthless topic. I don't think it is, but she might, and I don't want my grades to suffer." Ron had a flashback. *Did I dream that? Passions being squelched because of grades?* He couldn't shake the feeling, but he couldn't place it either.

"Well, I think you should write about what interests you. That's just my opinion, but let's see what we find in the barn, shall we?" Ron opened the barn doors, looked at Meghan and asked, "So what do you think?" He looked all around the massive space littered with relics from what could only be a hundred years or more. At least there seemed to be a hundred years of dust.

"Wow, there's a lot of stuff in here. I mean a *lot* of stuff."

"Well, all this over here is what we use to work the farm. You saw the tractor shed on the way here. All this stuff is for tending to the trees in the orchard and keeping the weeds at bay and of course picking all the apples. And that over there is where the livestock are when they're not outside. I always have a few goats. See them over there? Alright, alright," he said to the girls that knew it was feeding and milking time soon. "They produce the best goat cheese you ever tasted. The locals love it."

"Livestock?" Meghan asked.

"Sometimes I have a few steers or goats, like now, or pigs. It just depends on the prices and the futures of those commodities and what I need for myself," he said. "Sure, I live off of what I raise, but I send the rest to market." That was how he looked at things. The farm was a business and he was a businessman first. Meghan had no idea what he was talking about. That kind of language was something she never heard at home and certainly not in school. Didn't hear it on Instagram either.

"You mean you raise the livestock and then sell them for meat?" Meghan asked.

"Yes, or the cheese we make here with the goats. Or eggs. It's a very limited quantity, completely organic, and free-range so it commands a very high price. People buy what I sell because it says Orchard Canyon on it. They know the animals are treated right and are grass fed in the pasture."

"Kind of exclusive like designer handbags," Meghan said, rather shocked that her grandfather was the Louis Vuitton of Sedona for beef, chickens, eggs, and goat cheese.

"Yes, just like designer handbags," Ron was seeing that Meghan was catching on to the commerce model of this business called Orchard Canyon.

As Ron made his way to a far back corner, this time with Meghan behind him, he knew exactly what he wanted her to find. "This area back there, has a lot of stuff that has been there forever. Tractor parts, crates ... Let's see what we can find." Meghan had a look of sheer anticipation as she stepped over the old fence wire. Ron waited with anticipation. It was like when they would have family Easter egg hunts in the orchard. All the cousins would get together and when Ron blew the whistle, the search was on. He always wanted the kids to find a lot of eggs. Now he wanted Meghan to find his hidden treasure of old coins.

"Wow, check this out!" Meghan shouted as she spotted the pile of tractor parts covering the crate containing the old canning jar. Tickled, Ron just knew she had spotted the old jar. "Is this an old tractor seat?" Ron gave her a blank look. "Did people actually sit on this all day long?" She seemed shocked. Meghan had a rather sophisticated eye thanks to the Herman Miller ergonomically designed chairs that sat in her dad's home office and at her bedroom desk. Not to mention the exercise balls that so many people sat on at her mom's company. "Who would actually sit in this cold metal saddle and bump around all day in a field? This looks brutal!"

"Well, people did it. I did it way back when. It's what there was. What else do you see?" Ron changed the subject and hoped her attention would shift about a foot to the right.

"This looks cool." She found and picked up an old tin can with a lid. On it was a vintage looking Santa Claus image with two little kids in their pajamas looking wide-eyed. "Looks like something people would have used to store cookies back in the old days before plastic containers." Ron couldn't believe she missed the jar! Meghan was like a kid on Christmas morning eagerly trying to open the tin. When she did, she and Ron couldn't believe their eyes. Money! Old bills—fives, tens, twenties, maybe even hundreds. "Oh my gosh! Money? Is this really old money? It looks so different, but I recognize the faces on the bills."

Ron was stunned. How did he miss this? And how long had all this money been hidden in the corner of this barn? There had to be a thousand dollars in that tin! Clearly this was a Depression-era stash. There's no doubt now. After a quick look at the dates on a few bills the whole lot was of that era.

Chapter 11

Ron remembered what The Great Depression was like. He was born at the tail end and when he got a little older people were still scared and recovering. People his family knew lost everything and stopped trusting banks. Hundreds of banks went under. Depositors lost everything and they never got it back.

"Meghan, it looks like you stumbled upon a family secret. This would have been your great grandparents' way of saving the farm should the worst happen. My guess is they didn't trust the banks so they hid their money."

"What could happen?" Meghan asked.

"Well, during those times, people were really worried that the whole nation's economy would collapse. It almost did actually. People were out of work. There was no work on the farms, no work in the cities. The farms would produce goods, but there'd be no one to buy them. It was a real rough time."

"We just learned about the stock market crash of 1929 and how it caused the Depression. Was our family afraid? Were you afraid?" Meghan had never heard a first-hand account of The Great Depression, just what she had learned in text books and that was always pretty sanitized.

"Of course we were afraid. I mean I was just a little boy at the time. Judging from this can, I guess my parents were more afraid than even I thought, I mean given that my parents hid this money away." Ron actually was still in shock. "Your great grandfather was stoic. He never let on about anything, good or bad. We knew people in the cities were struggling. My parents would talk about it over dinner. And really it wasn't the stock market crash that killed things. It was overproduction of goods and not enough people to buy them. It was a worldwide thing. Everything stopped. When factories stopped producing cars because there weren't enough people to buy them, workers lost their jobs. That meant they didn't have money to buy shoes, so shoe factories closed. And those workers lost their jobs. And so it went. Like a house of cards."

"Wow, that's not how we learned it. But it makes more sense to me when you explain it like that." Meghan thought this was way more interesting than her history class. It was real.

"But Meghan, living on this farm, we didn't have it so bad. We always had food on our table. We grew our own and what extra we had, we'd sell on the corner at a vegetable stand. This tin might have been where they kept the money from the stand. Who knows?"

"Who could buy your vegetables if everyone was out of work?" Meghan was starting to catch onto this mini lesson about supply and demand.

"Well, here we had our own little economy. Still do to a degree. We weren't as reliant on the outside world like other cities and towns. People worked within the town and many didn't have enough money to put in banks, so they didn't lose their savings."

"And losing money in the stock market? We learned a lot of people lost money in the stock market. Just like in 2008." Meghan was seeing the parallels.

"Most people didn't have money invested in the stock market then. That was just for the rich people who felt that decline hard, but the rest of us didn't. In 2008, the Great Recession they call it, lots more people felt that one. Most people had money in the stock market because lots of people's retirement savings are in 401(k) plans which are mostly stocks." Meghan seemed interested in this little history lesson.

"Did *you* lose money in 2008?" Meghan asked

"No. No stock investments for me. Gave that up in the '80s. My investment is this place and all the businesses within it. The land, the orchards, the resort, the restaurant, the fruit stand, the meat and dairy—those signs that say 'orchard fresh apples' on the wall over there are to attract people to the fruit stand. This farm is a business, and a business is an investment. Sure, fewer people came and stayed here at the resort during those tough years, so our income was down. But we still had all the assets—the real estate, the orchards, the water from the creek, that's a huge asset too. Water in the West is valuable, more valuable than gold actually.

"I'm not like so many people who lost their jobs. Losing a job. That's what's really scary." Ron had no way of knowing that, in the midst of his history lesson about The Great Depression and more recently, the Great Recession, he had inadvertently touched on something very close to home: Meghan's dad, David, and his recent job loss.

By this point, Meghan knew what she was going to write her paper on. She was going to write about how people dealt with life in the Great Depression. Specifically, what they did when they were out of work, how they made ends meet, how they found new work—if they found it. She was all of a sudden interested in this subject. It was not only close to this home, having found the family rainy-day fund, but close to her own home. For the first time, she realized the significance of her dad being out of work. Suddenly her research about college tuition costs got a little more real.

Chapter 11

On the drive home, Meghan began to realize the difference between her mother and her father. Her mom was really more like her grandfather. She was a business owner too. And when she thought about it, her dad lost his job because of something that happened at work, but her mom and her grandfather didn't. And they never would.

Suddenly worried conversations between her mother and her father that she didn't understand as a young girl began to make sense. *Now I know why dad was so distant during the Great Recession. He was worried and probably scared because he was out of work then.* She saw the same behavior last weekend. Her dad was not himself. He was never a completely upbeat, positive person like her mom was, but he was clearly entering into that same low point Meghan now recognized from when she was just six or seven. She wondered if there was anything she and her grandfather could do to stop David from falling.

Chapter 12

"Hi, Dad. What's going on?" David was surprised to be receiving a text from his daughter at 12:15 on a Tuesday. But then again, any other week, she would likely not text for fear of disturbing him in a meeting.

"Hi, honey. Nothing much? You OK?" Seriously, the thought crossed his mind that something might be wrong.

"Yeah, I'm fine. Thought I'd come by after school. Got anything else going on?" David hated text shorthand and Meghan was better than most when he was texting her, forming almost complete sentences.

"Sure." He actually was embarrassed that he didn't have anything going on today or tomorrow or probably the next day. "What time? Should I pick up something for dinner?"

"I dunno, maybe 4. Mom wants me to meet her at Nola's for dinner, so I can't stay," Nola's was a chic gourmet burger joint in one of the hottest shopping districts on Camelback Road in Phoenix. "Wanna tell you about my visit with your dad." She still didn't quite know what to call Ron.

"Did you have a good time?"

"Yeah, great time. Tell you about it when I see you. Gotta run ... classes start soon."

David put his phone down and got back to what he was doing which was wondering what to do next. It was a fresh week of unemployment, and David had called everyone he kind of knew. The overwhelming response was they'd "Keep their eyes open," which usually meant, "don't hold your breath."

So he decided to call a few headhunters to let them know he was available. A few hours later without much progress, the door swung open and Meghan stormed in dropping her purse and backpack on the counter. "Hi, Dad! I'm here!"

"Hi, honey. How was your day?" he said, greeting her with a hug.

Meghan thought, *Hmm, he seems in higher spirits. Maybe he found a job!* Honestly, she had been worried about him since her visit to the farm. "My day was good. I'm excited because I told my history teacher my idea for my senior project and she really liked it. That's a huge relief!"

"Well, I can imagine. Grab yourself a soda from the fridge." Meghan walked over and got a Diet Coke, popped the top, and sat down at the counter. David grabbed one too along with a few cookies that were on the counter.

"So spill it. How was your visit with your grandfather? I still can't believe you went, considering how much you didn't want to go just a few weeks ago. But I'm glad." Part of David was glad, the other part was cautious. Especially after the college discussion last time they all were together.

"Well ..." Meghan lingered on that word. "I got there and couldn't wait to see what was in the barn. And you'll never believe what I found! I can't wait to tell you. I found an old Santa Claus tin with like at least a thousand dollars in it! Real old money."

David was stunned. "You found what?"

"I found a bunch of old money that we think belonged to my great grandparents who probably stashed it away when the banks all collapsed during The Great Depression."

Chapter 12

"The banks didn't *all* collapse, Meghan," David corrected, standing up a bit for the industry that left him temporarily high and dry. *How long is temporary?* he thought but didn't say.

"Yeah, whatever, but the point is, they hid all this money! No one knew it was there. We talked about how during that time, 'cause he was alive then, how lots of people lost their jobs and how living on that farm in the canyon wasn't nearly as scary as it was for people who worked in the cities. On the farm they always had food and a way to make money because they had the land. And that was worth something, plus it made money for the family. Kind of like Mom's business. Maybe you should think about starting a business rather than finding a job, Dad."

"I'm sure your grandfather made owning that little business up there sound like a dream come true. He has a way of glossing over things, in case you haven't noticed."

"I haven't noticed." Meghan felt like she needed to defend her grandfather from that last barb.

"Well, owning a business isn't easy. There's upkeep and costs, and employees and taxes. There's a lot to it. And some years it might not make any money."

Meghan interrupted, "Yes, actually, we talked about that. During the '70s things got rough because your dad had to take out some loans with really high interest." This was news to David. He had no idea.

"The point is, Meghan, when you work for a company, sure sometimes you're out of work like I am right now, but that's temporary." *Sooner rather than later, please*, he thought. "But you always get a paycheck. And you have benefits like health insurance and stock options, stuff like that."

"We learned people lost a lot of money in the stock market in 1929 and in 2008. Did you lose any?"

Kids have such a way of cutting right to the heart of the matter, David thought, but said, "Sure, everyone lost money. But it came back."

"Well, I think it was really hard on a lot of people back then, being out of work, especially, so I'm going to do my senior project on how people dealt with being out of work during The Great Depression. Did they find work, how did they go about it, did they start their own businesses? How did people survive?" Meghan asked, wondering what kind of response she would get.

"You're serious. Did you tell your grandfather about my situation?" David had to ask.

"No."

"Okay, well good. Because this is just temporary." David hoped.

"I know. But we're invited back this Sunday for dinner and I said we'd come." Just as she was breaking that news, her phone buzzed. It was her mom texting, "Are you on your way?"

"What?" David said, a little peeved.

"We're going. I'll drive. It'll be great. I gotta go. Mom will kill me if I'm late." A quick hug, and Meghan grabbed her stuff and was out the door.

CHAPTER 13

"This is my favorite part of the drive. I love Cathedral Rock. I want to come up here and hike it sometime," Meghan said as she steered the car past the Back O' Beyond area entering into the town of Sedona. She glanced to her left at the towering red rocks that looked more like art sculptures than natural geological formations.

Meghan and her dad were on their way up to Orchard Canyon for Sunday dinner. Meghan was so excited. She had a lot on her list for her visit. She wanted to ask her dad a few questions for her project and see what else she could discover in the treasure trove in her grandfather's property.

"Yeah, that would be good exercise; it's not as easy as it looks. I hiked it many, many years ago," David said making conversation and looking on his phone at the Job Postings for the week and his emails to see if anyone replied back to his asks for contacts who may be able to lead him to his next job. They were about fifteen minutes away, not counting traffic from Orchard Canyon. Fifteen minutes until he would be dodging questions like, "How's it going?"

When Meghan turned into the Orchard Canyon drive and crossed Oak Creek, she caught a glimpse of the cabins that were nestled in the woods with the towering canyon as a backdrop. Ron was right near the gate, fixing one of the posts that was looking a little crooked. "Hey, here they are! Just pull on through." Ron followed as the car eased through the narrow gate and into the parking area.

"Hi, Dad, nice to see you," David said as he exited the car. Megan was gathering her purse and her iPad that held her senior project thus far and, of course, unplugging her phone. She got out of the car and yelled out, "Hi!!!"

"Hi, Meghan!" Ron greeted her with a big smile, and a hug. "Do you need me to carry anything?"

"Yeah, thanks," Meghan said, handing Ron her backpack.

"Come on in, you two." They walked toward the main house and into the kitchen.

"So, how's it going? Meghan, did you have a good week?" Ron asked as he poured some warm, mulled cider into cups.

"It smells like apples in here," David said. "Reminds me of when I was a kid." *When things were easier,* he thought.

As if there were two conversations going on, Meghan replied, "My week was good. My history teacher loved my idea for my project. It's going to be about how people in the Depression got along being out of work and how they found new jobs or even started businesses. I think it's going to be interesting."

"How much cider are the orchards producing now, Dad?" David was wondering because he was curious—and because he wanted to do a little math related to how much revenue the cider operation was bringing in.

"Then the teacher told me that this was one of the most original projects she ever heard of. I didn't let her know about the thousand dollars of old money we found. I didn't want to ruin the secret!"

"We're producing about four-thousand cases of cider a year. Not nearly enough to meet the demand. There are a lot of places, you know, local stores, and even restaurants asking for us to supply them.

We have a good name. But I just don't have anyone right now to take on sourcing quality apples beyond what we grow, negotiating the business side of these wholesale arrangements or production. You know what it takes. It's a lot of work." he replied to David. Then to Meghan, "That's wonderful, Meghan! Yeah, don't let them in on that little find yet. You're smart." Then addressing them both, "Hey, dinner's ready. I hope you're hungry."

When they sat down they took the same seats in the kitchen as they had the last time the three were all together. "Dinner looks like a winner, dad," David said as he cut into a lean piece of piping hot pot roast. This is so different than the life David was living. The early Sunday dinner was something he remembered from his childhood, but who actually did that anymore, with families all running in 15 different directions at all times?

"So, about that thousand dollars we found—did Meghan tell you?" Ron asked David.

"She said you found some money, and that it was old, but that's about it," David replied, actually wondering if Meghan did say more and he just forgot. This whole job thing and the debt thing were looming large. He was still out of it.

"It was so cool finding that cookie tin, plus we found a jar filled with old coins. Did I tell you that? A lot of them were real silver, Dad," Meghan chimed in between bites of the potatoes that were cooked alongside the pot roast in the oven. "We think that was a rainy-day fund, and a thousand dollars was a lot of money way back then."

"Speaking of a thousand dollars, I was watching CNN the other day and there was a story about how most people today don't even have a thousand dollars to their name. They've barely saved a dime! All those big salaries, what are they doing with their money?" Ron asked in disbelief at the statistic he heard. "Isn't this amazing to you, David? You work for a bank."

Meghan shot a glance at her dad, as if to ask, *Are you going to tell him?* She got her answer pretty quickly.

"Well, Dad, I don't actually work in consumer banking and even if I did, I wouldn't see everyone's bank accounts or balances," replied David, attempting to neutralize the conversation. Even Meghan could detect the evasiveness in her dad's reply. What she didn't know was that that same news story was weighing heavily on David's mind, because his own finances weren't very far off from that statistic.

"Well, I think it is downright irresponsible that people overspend like that," Ron said.

Meghan actually could relate because she knew very well that a thousand dollars didn't buy much at her favorite store. *I mean it's like a pair of designer boots, a sweater and a pair of okay jeans. That's a thousand dollars,* she thought, contemplating that she actually had never seen a thousand dollars in bills until finding the tin in the barn. "That's the first time I had ever seen that much money," Meghan piped in. "I mean in cash. I use a credit card and Mom showed me how we get cash back for every dollar we spend. That's a good deal, isn't it?"

"It's a good deal if you want to reward irresponsible spending," Ron answered as he served himself another helping of salad. "Years ago, *saving* was rewarded. Not today—it's *spending* that earns you money, but you never get ahead. You can't spend your way to saving money."

David didn't really want to go into the way credit cards worked, and that the American economy and therefore the world was based on consumer spending and debt. Debt *is* money which is hard for most people to comprehend. But think of it this way: when someone owes you a debt, that is an asset that has value to you the person who lent it because the borrower will pay you back in full plus interest.

Fail to pay the loan and you get to take possession of whatever asset has secured the loan as collateral. That's a good deal. That's how banks make money and right now they make a lot of money on credit card debt.

"Dad, consumer spending is what keeps the world going around and America on top," David tried to simplify his thoughts thinking his dad might not understand. "The more debt, the more money in the system. Money is created through debt."

"I thought all the money was in Fort Knox. No, I mean all the gold that backs the money. Fort Knox must be huge! There's a lot of money around. I hear it on the news. One fighter plane costs billions of dollars. That's a lot of gold bars," said Meghan.

"Honey, gold doesn't back money anymore. That ended in the '70s, way before you were born," David clarified. "What are they teaching you in that school you're attending? I hope you're listening in class."

"I listen. But we don't really talk about money at all. We talk about history. If money isn't gold, then what is it?" Meghan looked confused and confounded. "Silver?"

Ron jumped in, surprising David, "Meghan, today money is just the paper or metal it's minted with. It's just currency that is used to buy things. The more you have of it, the wealthier you are. The less you have, the poorer. But the dollar, it's not backed by anything."

"So, how is all this money created? Where does it come from?" Meghan was clearly shocked.

"Thin air," Ron responded spontaneously with a bit of an attitude. You could tell he had an opinion about this.

"It's not thin air, Dad. Meghan, world banks decide when the economy would benefit from more money being added to it—"

"So people can borrow it and spend more and get into more debt," Ron interrupted.

David threw a look at his father, who clearly was trying to corrupt the child, then continued, "World banks decide when more money is needed for the economy and they create it by loaning governments money who can then print it as currency."

"That's how the government buys the billion-dollar fighter plane without having any gold in Fort Knox." Meghan was catching on.

"Well yes, that is correct, and ..."

“But, Meghan, it’s also what causes governments and people to be in such deep debt that they will never dig out of it,” Ron said.

“And ... it’s this infusion of money—capital—into the economy that allows the company that builds those planes to hire people and pay them wages. It keeps people employed,” David paused and even Meghan saw the irony in what he just said.

So, why did you get fired if there’s all this money? she thought but didn’t dare say.

“Let me clarify something, Meghan. All that is fine if, and only if, the money that is spent is invested, meaning it provides income. Those boots you’re wearing. How’d you pay for them?

“With a credit card,” Meghan said matter of factly.

“Do you pay off your credit card every month?” Ron asked looking at Meghan.

“Do we pay our credit card off every month, Dad?” Meghan asked bouncing the question to her father.

“No, we don’t. We have a float for cash flow purposes.” David was getting aggravated.

"Whatever you want to call it," Ron said. Then turning to Meghan, "Do those boots make you money when you wear them?"

"No," Meghan said laughingly. "How would they make me money?" Meghan thought her grandfather was kidding.

"What if you spent that money on say, an iPad? Could an iPad make you money?" Ron asked.

"Well … I guess so."

"Why? What could you do with it?"

"Ummm, I could use it to sell stuff online I guess," Meghan responded. "I get it. Like Mom does."

"Exactly. It can make you a producer of something that others can buy. That's why the debt of buying an iPad that you use to make money is an investment. And those boots are just an expense. They make you a consumer, not a producer. Too many consumer expenses with too much debt and you go bankrupt,"

"I get it. So Mom with her company is a producer."

"Yes! You're getting it, now. Orchard Canyon is a producer and a producer with multiple ways to make money is always more stable and safe than a person with only one source of income."

Ron just delivered a very hard-hitting lesson on how money works and how it doesn't. He delivered a lesson on entrepreneurship and how today, just like during the Great Depression, making money any way you can and watching your expenses was the best approach to attaining security and wealth.

David shifted in his chair and thought this conversation needed to shift to the peach pie that was on the counter. "Hey you guys, that pie and ice cream isn't going to serve itself. Who's ready for something sweet?"

Chapter 14

CHAPTER 14

Jon Trayler. The name, a blast from the past appeared on David's cell phone. *At last,* he thought, *one of my better job leads calling me back.* David breathed a sigh of relief or apprehension, he wasn't sure which. Thankfulness, and desperation both resided in the same gulp of air. "Jonny! How's it going?" David blurted his best confident-guy greeting, hoping it masked his fear without being overly amped up, "It's been way too long. What, two or three years? I think the last time we talked you were heading up the trust department at First National." *God, there's not even a First National anymore,* David thought. That merger happened five, maybe six years ago.

"Hi, David, and I guess we need to get you a watch or a calendar or something. It's got to be at least six years. I've had three jobs since First National! How the heck are you? It was great to hear from you," David's ego felt a little bruised, then recovered when Jon actually sounded glad for the call.

"So what's going on? Where are you now?" David asked, hoping it was somewhere that he wanted to work, that maybe was looking for talent, and that could bring him on, say ... Monday.

Don't get your hopes up, David's voice of self-doubt became the third person in the conversation.

"Oh, gosh. Well, you know, I left First National. Things started getting a little crazy over there with the new management after the merger. It was horrible. All the perks? Gone. So from there I moved over to the Trust Department—Private Client banking for Citi. Stayed there for about a year, got a few more letters after my name, they paid for them (thank you very much), and thought, it's time I move into a real financial services role rather than banking. I was going nowhere."

"Wow, that sounds great, really great," David said. But it didn't sound great. His banking contact, the one he was banking on, was no longer in banking. Ugh! "So where are you then?"

"Oh, yeah, that's what you asked me. Ha! Same old me, getting sidetracked. So now I'm an analyst with E-Trade. No more selling. No more dealing with customers. I do the monitoring, tracking, and analysis to figure out where the company should move assets next. It's a 60-hour work week, but the Ph.D. is paying off. I just took delivery on my new Maserati. Remember how I said I always wanted one? My wife's pissed as hell, but you can't have everything perfect, right?"

How could a call go so wrong so fast?, David wondered It was like the whole world had moved on and moved up while he was stuck at the bank, buried in the vault. While he was clawing from the upper tier of middle management or the lower tier of upper management, others were taking risks. His own ex-wife included. Even his father, by expanding the family orchards into a vacation getaway for Arizona tourists. And now Jon. Doing the work for a Ph.D.? Wow.

"So what's going on with you? You said you had some big news."

Not knowing where to start, and not recalling saying he had "big" news, David attempted to get the facts out without seeming desperate. "Well, I'm in the midst of a transition too. Maybe where you were several years back. I left the bank and am out looking for my next gig."

Jon quickly blurted with disbelief, "You quit before you had another job?"

"No-no, no, we had a reorganization and it was part of that."

"Wow, sorry, David," suddenly things got more somber which made David feel even more apprehensive. Did Jon think he was never going to find a job? "Hey, I have to get going here, but maybe we could grab a beer later today? Whadya' say? Probably would be good to catch up. The markets close in about three hours, meet you at Chelsea's?"

"Yeah, that sounds great, actually. I'll be there." David was once again hopeful. He couldn't believe how lonely he must actually be. He couldn't wait to get back out into the real world, with a real world colleague and be ... normal.

Three hours later, by the time David pulled up to the parking lot, he saw Jon getting out of his new Maserati. "Hey, nice car!" David shouted out of his window as he drove by. "I'll park and meet you in there," he said with a chuckle. *Nice car, no kidding*, he thought.

The hostess greeted David with a smile maybe a little wider than normal as he walked in. Just for a moment he had that familiar feeling of confidence. *I still got it*, he thought. *But you're still not working,* his nagging voice interrupted.

"I see my buddy right over there, thanks," and he quickly made his way into the bar.

"There you are, thanks for getting together. This is great. Beer?"

"Beer. Blue Moon ... bottle." After a little more small talk, David thought it was time to get to the point. "So, I've been looking around and the job well is coming up dry. Know anyone who's hiring?"

"Man, I don't. And our firm, I don't know if you'd find anything you really would want to do. You'd have to take some backward steps," Jon said. "I mean, it's great and I'm grateful for the salary and bonus, but, truthfully, David, I feel like I sold my soul to the devil. I work all the time, never see my kids. Look at me. I have to be forty pounds heavier since I saw you last. I haven't worked out in years ..."

For the first time in a while, David actually felt sorry for someone other than himself. Jon needed someone to talk with. He remembered that life well, the toll it took on his relationships and his health. The weight gain creep, a few pounds every year. And now, David was clamoring to get back into it? How many days did he say to himself that he wanted out of it when he was in it? A lot. What was he thinking? Jon was continuing his picture of reality while David was coming to grips with his own confusion.

"... My doctor's telling me if I keep eating all this crappy fast food, or just as bad, all this ultra rich food, I'm going to need a triple bypass. Me? A triple bypass! But who has time to eat healthy? I'm never home. Even today, I have to go back to the office before going home ..."

Oh, my Lord. Jon is me, David thought. *The former you,* that voice corrected and David replied, *Thank God, for former. Do I really want to get back into this crazy life of feeling in control, but not being in control?*

"... I'm making more money than ever," Jon continued, "but I have nothing but a bunch more stuff to show for it. My own investments haven't even kept up with the market. I'm just saying, you getting out might have been a blessing in disguise. Think long and hard, my friend, about what you want to do. As much as I don't like being out of work, I kind of envy you. You have a chance to reinvent yourself." Jon took the last swig of his beer, promised to keep in touch and quickly dashed out. He had four hours' worth of work to do and it was already 5:30.

David sat on the barstool. He felt awakened to the reality of his former life, and shocked by his own insanity of lamenting it. *Why would you want to throw yourself back on the hamster wheel?* he thought. He compared the frenzy of the past hour to the solitude of Orchard Canyon, the place and the business. *Can business really be like that? Profitable and sane? High on opportunity and low on sacrifice?*

Finishing his beer, he looked around. He saw the people, the patio, the mountains in the sunset. And he thought, *This is Phoenix, the place that when I got here from my small home town to the north felt like the land of opportunity. This is still Phoenix and opportunity is everywhere. That's what Arizona is all about. I'm just turning over one rock and there are millions of rocks. Huge ones. I have to be open to turning over a few new ones. Taking a different trail.*

At that moment, that feeling of life being better in Arizona than anywhere else started to return. He didn't realize that feeling had been missing in action for so long. He felt the sides of his lips turn up a bit for the first time in a long time. He began to believe in the magic of this place, and the destiny it could hold at this time in his life.

Chapter 15

CHAPTER 15

"You're in a good mood this morning," David said when Meghan lightly trotted from her room to the kitchen. "You excited to be going shopping with Mom today?"

"Well, yeah. But you made pancakes!" David was clearly in a better state of mind after his beer with an angel named Jon. He even made breakfast. "When was the last time you made pancakes?" David couldn't remember.

"Well, too long," he answered. "One, two, or three?" And just went ahead and piled three on Meghan's plate without waiting for her reply. "Syrup's on the table."

"These smell great, Dad. Mmmmm ... and they taste great. Looove pancakes!" She was almost singing like she used to when she was a little kid eating something reeeeeaally good. David smiled to himself. This was the best he felt since this whole job thing. Maybe even before that.

David served himself a stack of three and joined Meghan at the table. Meghan could tell her dad was having a good day. “I thought I would drop you off at your mom’s today a little before noon. She’s been wanting to get my opinion on a few business loan questions, so I thought today is as good a day as any. Shouldn’t take long and you will still have plenty of time to head out to the mall.”

“Dad, no one goes to the mall anymore. We’re going to Fashion Square,” the teen in Meghan showing itself through the ample amount of sugary maple syrup in her plate.

“Well, pardon me,” David said jokingly. “I stand corrected by the master!”

“You’re in a good mood today, too,” Meghan said. She didn’t like to see her dad struggling and knew he was, even if she didn’t fully understand all the reasons why. This was honestly the first good day in weeks, and she couldn’t really remember him ever being like this, even when he was working. Somehow he was different.

After breakfast and the dishes were cleaned up, David and Meghan each went their separate ways to get ready for the day. David retreated into the master bedroom he shared with no one and dropped down on the floor and attempted to knock out 50 push-ups. He got to 16 and collapsed. The reality of change, of transformation was going to be brutal. *I may as well brace myself. When have you ever known change to be easy, David?* he asked himself looking in the mirror and seeing the paunch he'd been cultivating for at least 10 years.

Time flies when you're 16 getting ready to go shopping. You have to make sure you look good, otherwise how can the clothes you try on look good on you? Meghan had 10 minutes before she had to leave and her hair was still soaking wet. With the blow dryer motor whining, Meghan began thinking about what it must be like for her dad. He hasn't seen anyone he worked with in a long time. *That might be kind of like not being able to see my friends at school,* she thought. And even though some of the people at school weren't necessarily people she liked hanging out with, the thought of not being included made her feel lonely. *That's got to be how Dad feels.*

The truth was, David did miss his work community. That was part of his loss when he lost his job. Everyone needs a community. "Meghan, you almost ready?" David called.

"Almost, Dad. Two minutes," with her new-found empathy for her dad's reality, she cut him a break and didn't impatiently bark her response in classic teenage style. "Coming right out ..."

As Meghan crossed the family room, David couldn't help speaking his mind, "Well, you look lovely." His daughter was growing up, had grown up, and he was just noticing it for the first time.

"Thank you, but I look just like I did yesterday, Dad," she said, awkwardly deflecting the compliment.

"You looked lovely then, too. Ready to go?"

The two hopped into the Beemer and drove from the big Scottsdale house to Susan's smaller one in the historic district in Phoenix. When Susan and David divorced, the financial part of it was easy. Susan was starting her company and needed all the cash she could get. They split up their retirement accounts and the small amount of cash they had on hand. For all the success that David had had to that point, they didn't have a lot to show for it. He took out a second mortgage on the big house to pay Susan her portion of the equity.

That cash was enough for Susan to buy a fixer-upper in a neighborhood she always thought was kind of hip, but borderline seedy. David didn't like the idea of her moving out of the safe Scottsdale city limits, but he had no say in the matter. At that point in the divorce he was just ready for a little peace. It was tumultuous for a while.

Susan put an offer on a 1948 bungalow in the Green Gables Historic District of Phoenix. David took a Saturday afternoon and drove by. He thought the place was a mess. Susan thought it was a diamond in the rough. They disagreed on just about everything; why should this have been any different? And as crazy as it sounds, David had been back there only one time since. That was just a few months after Susan had moved in, to drop off a photo of her grandmother she had left at the Scottsdale house. That was it. David always meant to stop by once the wounds of their breakup began to heal, but one thing led to another, he was just too busy. And with Meghan getting her license that year, that pretty much meant she could drive herself between her parents' homes.

"Wait till you see what Mom's house looks like, Dad." Meghan was reading David's mind. "You aren't going to believe it."

"I recall it was quite a dump even a year or so ago. I know you didn't like staying there much. But you haven't complained in a while. I'm going to take that as a good sign." David really was hopeful because he wanted the best for Susan even though he had a habit of not showing it.

Chapter 15

"It's a very good sign. It's really cool." Meghan said as David rounded the corner onto Garfield Road and five houses in he hardly recognized the place. He hardly recognized the neighborhood! Even he had to admit the character of the neighborhood was striking. Quaint gingerbread-style roof lines on adobe exterior walls with wood trim, front porches with old-fashioned wood-worked railings. The place looked like a storybook. And plenty of expensive cars in driveways. Clearly the neighborhood had transitioned since the last time he was there.

David pulled the car in front and Meghan looked at him. She could tell he was shocked. "I told you! Isn't it amazing?" She grabbed her things, jumped out of the car and instantly transformed from teenager going shopping with Mom to HGTV home improvement show host. "Remember this over here, Dad? This was where that craggy old palm tree was. Well, they took a big truck and pulled it out of the ground and that's how come you can see the 1940's style bungalow roof line and the front porch that's perfect for entertaining."

"1940's-style .... Bungalow ... Roof line ... Entertaining ... Who are you, Meghan?" David was both kidding and serious at the same time.

"Quit it, Dad," Meghan said, laughing, knowing she truly did sound like one of the twins on "The

Property Brothers" TV show. "Wait until you see inside." Meghan bounded up the porch steps across the plank floor and opened the front door. David stood back a bit, not feeling comfortable just walking into his ex-wife's home. Susan came to the door to greet Meghan and was surprised to see David standing at the bottom of the porch steps.

"Hi, honey." Susan hugged Meghan and ushered her in. "David, what a surprise."

"Hi, Susan. I thought I'd drop Meghan off and go over those few loan document questions you had. I mean if now is a good time. If it's not, that's okay. I have other stuff I need to do. I can come back," It was awkward. Why was it awkward? It's not awkward on the phone anymore.

"Of course, that would be so wonderful if you could help me with that today. I just know you are more experienced with the nuances of commercial loans, and I think I can trust you." She glanced back, "I'm kidding. C'mon in."

David walked onto the porch and was absolutely charmed by the beautiful mid-century-modern lines of the furniture. Susan saw him looking at the painted steel rocking chairs. "Those are the real deal, David. A friend of mine found them at a flea market and said I had to have them. They were a mess when he dropped them off, but with a little work and a lot of paint, voilà!"

"Very nice, Susan," David said almost absent-mindedly as he continued to shift his gaze all around the exterior of the house. Meghan was frantically signaling to her dad to come in so she could do her HGTV host shtick. He barely noticed.

"Dad, get in here!"

"Okay, okay," David finally made his way back from his stupor and walked into the house. *How did she do this?* he thought. And run a company. And have Meghan here most of the time. And ... What have *I* done since our divorce?

With Meghan's tour well underway, Susan began to share how she really has gotten the bug for taking old Phoenix homes, fixing them up and in some cases renting them, in other cases selling them. Over the last two years, she's done a few thanks to a realtor who helps her find her ugly duckling houses, a team of great guys who help her turn them into swans, and an interior design friend who does the work at a discount in exchange for Susan's houses being her real-life portfolio.

"I have three rental houses now, all redone, and with wonderful tenants," said Susan. "I thought you knew I was doing this," Susan could tell by

David's stunned look that he had no idea. All he kept thinking was, while she went out and bought this old fixer-upper, he went out and bought a shiny new boat. The boat hasn't been in the water for over a year, nowhere near water and was in need of a lot of maintenance. It's worth half or less of what he paid for it. Susan had a house that was badly in need of repair and now ...

"I looked on Zillow, Dad. This house is worth almost half a million dollars!" Meghan finished his sentence. Susan paid $98,000 for it. He remembered the number well. It was the same price as his boat. David began to see his life choices for what they were. He had bought Meghan's boots and Susan had bought the iPad. Actually, three iPads and they were all generating money. *If I had a few income-earning properties right now, things would be so much less stressful*, he thought.

"Susan, I'm really impressed by all you have done. This place," glancing around, "it's beautiful. And three rental properties, plus a business. That's awesome." he paused, a bit timid about asking the next question. But he had to know. "How did you do all this?"

"Really, David? You know how I did it. I worked constantly on the business when we were together. When you were at the office or out schmoozing clients,

I was working at home and then on the weekends, I started looking at houses. My little addiction is paying off."

David was starting to realize that his secure life, the life he preached as gospel for "how it is done," was looking more and more like one big illusion. And what he thought was risky, starting a business and buying inner-city real estate, actually wasn't. He had followed the prescription everyone did. Was it everyone? How could being part of the status quo be so wrong?

"So, David, the reason I wanted to talk with you," Susan said, "is to ask about alternative finance options other than traditional mortgages. I have assets now—my other rental houses, my business, my personal house, some equities. And I'd like to know if there is a better way to fund my next rental house. I really think it's time to acquire another one. I have the cash."

"It wouldn't take me long to just do some quick calculations if you want to look at it all now," David said. He did want to help, but he was also dying to know how well she was doing. He wanted to know how and when she started to really see her efforts pay off. What did the trajectory look like? And what's it look like now?

Susan had three rental properties worth a combined $750,000 and her own house worth almost $500,000. That was $1,250,000 in real estate value. “Susan, how much do you owe on your real estate?”

“About $50,000,” Susan answered.

“On which property? What about the others?” David asked.

“That’s the total. I only owe money on one of the properties,” Susan said. She continued, “The rentals are driving about $5,000 per month in income.” David was envious of his own ex-wife.

Having learned through a few other questions that she was also sitting on approximately $300,000 in cash, it became clear that she could easily get a loan with the rental properties as collateral. She could use a small amount of her cash as a down payment and make money renting the new house. “Susan, based on your financial position, there are some favorable lending options that are open to you. You have done amazingly well.” David was happy for her.

Chapter 16

CHAPTER 16

David spent the next two days trying to figure out how his ex-wife's financial picture took such a positive path while his own took such a negative one. Obviously, his loss of income made the jagged cliff he had been living on far more tenuous. And it was no wonder that, when they split the assets in the divorce, Susan had said, "No, you keep the boat and the big house." She didn't want them. She knew they were liabilities. The boat, of course, was expensive to maintain and store. And the house had a high mortgage on it thanks to that expensive remodel. Just when the mortgage was getting to a reasonable level, they had decided the house needed a facelift. *That was a mistake*, David thought.

He also thought he might need some professional help. *When was the last time I spoke to a financial advisor?* The last time he could recall was in a casual conversation with one of the guys who advised customers in the bank trust department where he worked. They were both getting coffee in the break room This guy's job was to sell investments like mutual funds to the bank's wealthier depositors. He targeted people with large savings or checking accounts and steered them toward investments that had the potential to pay more interest.

The investments are riskier and the principal is not guaranteed like it is in savings accounts, certificates of deposit, or money market accounts. With banks paying pitiful interest rates that don't even come close to keeping up with inflation, you lose buying power every year you keep your money in one of those vehicles. If inflation is 3 percent and your money market is making 1.5 percent, you lose 1.5 percent of every dollar you have. So, a dollar, after a year is really only 85 cents. Keep that up and you end up poor. As he thought about it, *I remember my savings account when I was in high school. It was paying 9 percent interest. That's about the stock market average, but with no risk. Too bad inflation was 14 percent at the time. Bank savings accounts are misnamed,* he thought.

Figuring out what to do with his money wasn't David's problem, however. He didn't have much cash left. What he did have was a 401(k) retirement account through his former company. He figured he had 10 more years or so to work, if he was lucky. And he would need money to retire. He was pretty sure he didn't have enough in his retirement account to live his current lifestyle for any length of time, even if that money had 10 more years to grow. And that's hoping the economy stayed strong. His entire retirement account was in stocks.

David picked up the phone and made an appointment with Roger Foster, a financial advisor a friend had recommended at least two years ago. His friend said, "This guy made me a bunch of money. You have to call him." David never did. He never really had any money to invest, with all the expenses he and Susan had when they were married. Now he was calling not about investing, but to get a reality check on his next 10 years. David was dreading the meeting, but couldn't put it off any longer.

"Hello, Roger. Yes, I was calling because a friend of mine and client of yours, Ray Cassel, suggested I talk with you. I'm looking for some retirement planning."

"Excellent, yes, of course I know Ray. And I'm your guy for retirement planning. Before I set you up on the calendar, let me ask just a few questions. How old are you?"

"I'm 57," David replied.

"And how long before you want to retire?"

"Let's say 10 years."

"And do you know how much money you have slated to invest over that period?" This guy obviously asked them these questions a thousand times before.

"Well, I have a 401(k) worth about $400,000."

"Any new money to add to that?" Again asking very matter of factly, like he was checking the boxes on a form.

"No, not really at this time..." this question wasn't easy for David to answer. He knew what was coming next.

"Our minimum for taking on clients is really $1 million and up. But because you're a friend of Ray's, I'll see what we can do. I mean, at least I can give you some advice. Will Thursday work for you?"

David felt desperate. "Yes, that will work."

When Thursday rolled around, David was all nerves. His stomach felt queasy and he couldn't eat. So he downed a second cup of coffee which wasn't the best choice, and headed out the door. As he got into the Beemer, he noticed that his tires were looking a little worn. Actually, more than a little worn. *God, another thing! I'm going to need all new tires here. I need them now! But that's at least $1,500 I don't have! What next?*

As he got in the car, David's adrenaline was running high—fight or flight mixed with caffeine—and he could feel it. Sweat beaded up on his forehead. He wiped it with his hand and started the car. "Let's see, I'm heading to 32nd Street and Camelback Road in Phoenix ..." David said to no one as he backed out the car. His cell phone connected to the car audio system and the first song that he heard was George Thorogood and the Delaware Destroyers' *One Bourbon, One Scotch, One Beer*, which is a song about a guy who loses his job, can't find another one, and gets kicked out of his apartment. "Not today," David said as he quickly turned off the music and put on KFNN, the Money station. That song was a favorite during his college days and it usually brought back fond memories. Today it was a reminder of his current state of life. *Even listening to the crazy stuff happening on Wall Street is better than that,* he thought.

He learned Apple shares were up .01 percent, Cisco was down .02 percent on light trading. The radio show host was speculating where interest rates were going and how a 25-basis-point-move would impact the markets. Same old, same old, then a bunch of commercials. When the host returned, as David was nearing the intersection of Lincoln Drive and Tatum Road in Paradise Valley, it was time for the Wall Street Winners segment of his show. That's where the host runs through the list of high flyers that everyone wished they owned. The top performer was some obscure highly leveraged genomics company which was up as much at 120 percent for the year so far and had no profits. David couldn't help but fantasize how all his troubles would be over if he had his retirement account in that stock. Of course, that's not the way investing works. It's all about diversifying, because that one stock could just as easily fall 75 percent because of a product defect, market softening, or investors finally realizing the company has no earnings.

David was certain this advisor was going to look at his financial picture and tell him there was nothing he could do. With a file folder in hand containing his most recent quarterly investment statements and a spreadsheet of his current assets and liabilities, David climbed out of the car, glanced at his left front tire, and kept walking toward the office building door. A quick look at the building directory and an elevator ride to the fourth floor, David was where he really didn't want to be: Walking into a financial advisor's office. "I'm here to see Roger Foster."

"Yes, we are expecting you. Please take a seat in the lobby. Roger will be right in." The offices were beautiful. They looked like a Ralph Lauren ad with dark wood paneling and leather furniture. Bookshelves with richly-bound books no one ever read. "By the way, is your wife named Susan?"

"Yes ... well, my ex-wife."

"I just read about her amazing story in the *Phoenix Business Journal*. So interesting how she helps budding fashion designers get discovered. And I checked the website. There are some fabulous clothes there. What a great idea for a business." David took a seat and assured the receptionist, "I'll let her know she has another fan." He felt out of his element and didn't really need the reminder that Susan was excelling and he was not.

"Hi. You must be David. I'm Roger Foster."

"Pleased to meet you, Roger." David replied, wondering whether he really would be pleased in about 20 minutes. "Looks like we both know Ray Cassel." The two sat down and Roger proceeded to jump right to questions of substance about David's current state of financial affairs. David started to wonder how well Roger really knew Ray. Probably not that well.

"I brought my current investment statements and my financial records. I should tell you I am between jobs right now and a little concerned about money. I'm really hoping you can help me get a better picture of my present as well as my future." The meeting started out rough. Roger continued to ask hard and sometimes embarrassing questions. He clearly had a process he took everyone through.

David discovered that even with very optimistic projections of his current investments, he would not be in a position to retire at age 67 or at all, and still maintain his lifestyle for more than a year or two. He also learned that within the next three months, David would have to find a job or begin taking money out of his retirement plan to pay for living expenses. That would not only be a blow to his financial security, but also a tax and penalty hit that the advisor could not recommend. "Find a job, David, anything at this point that can help make ends meet. You're teetering really close to having to make some really hard choices."

Then this advisor suggested he roll his current retirement account into a new strategy that had performed better over the last five years than his current fund had. Some advisors based future performance on past performance. *Does that make sense?* David wondered. *Doesn't matter, his recommendations would end up costing me more money in fees, and that's not an option.* I guess Roger thought he was due some sort of commission since he did the retirement analysis for free. David left a bit smarter, but didn't like being "sold" as a conclusion to the meeting. Roger, it turned out, was a salesman who made money when he sold something. He wasn't a true advisor who made money when he helped his clients make money. "Roger is not my guy," David said aloud as he backed out of the parking lot.

By the end of the day, David had arrived at the conclusion that some big life changes were inevitable. He wasn't sure what they were, but there was no doubt. *I can't keep going like I have been. I've got to make some changes. I've got to get my head on straight here. Stop feeling defeated, David. Move on. Move forward. Pick yourself up.*

The internal pep talk seemed to help a bit. He got on the phone and while on his way home tried to set up some more meetings with headhunters. But every time he dialed the cell service got sketchy and the phone dropped the call. *Just drive, David.* That seemed to be the message.

Chapter 17

Chapter 17

"Dad finally saw Mom's house," Meghan blurted out as she burst into Ron's house, dropped her purse, and ran into the kitchen. "I kept telling him all the cool things she was doing with it and it was like he was too busy to care."

"I wasn't too busy to care. It just wasn't a priority, but I'm glad you gave me the tour," David said. "Susan did a really nice job. And she's doing things, investing in properties, in her business that ... well, I'm impressed with how well they're doing. How well she's doing."

"Well, they say seeing is believing, but in this case maybe believing is seeing." Ron let that tidbit of wisdom hang in the air, not knowing if Meghan was old enough yet, or David open-minded enough, to understand that we have to believe in something before it can become real and we can see it. People who wait to see before they believe miss out.

"Well, Susan believed in her dream and she believed she could do it. So she's living it. That's how I see it," Ron said. "Talk about seeing, have either of you ever seen pictures of Orchard Canyon from way back when my parents owned it, and even before?"

"You have pictures? No way! Maybe I can use them in my project. I just learned Thursday that we have to do a presentation, too. I was just going to take some pictures of the old money we found and where we found it, but now I can show the old farm, too. Awesome! I feel an A coming my way!"

"I'll let you two look at old pictures, and Meghan I'm glad you're shooting for an A. According to Dad, you'll get it so long as you believe," David said.

"And put the work in. Let's not forget that part," Ron said.

Meghan was excited and no wonder. This was the first time she actually had a sense of history in her life. Of where she came from. It was the first time that she was actually seeing something more vivid of her past than her parents' wedding photos that once graced the mantle of their home but were seldom ever seen, really. They, like so many fixtures in the house, were simply that. Fixtures that had stories behind them, but were never told. It was her first sense of history beyond her own baby pictures and the funny stories of her toddler years. There's probably not a person alive who doesn't like hearing funny stories about their childhood.

"Come with me. We have a few hours before dinner's ready. That will give us a lot of time to explore," Ron said and he led Meghan to the attic storage room. As they were walking down the hall toward the the ladder they'd use to climb into the attic, Meghan and Ron approached two bedrooms, one on each side of the second-floor hall. Meghan had never been upstairs in this house. Ron pointed to the farthest bedroom and said, "That was your father's room. He shared it with his brother."

"Really!" Meghan couldn't help but quicken her step and get there first. Then with her hand on the doorknob about ready to open the door, she launched a polite glance back at Ron and said, "Mind?"

"Go ahead. Take a look."

Meghan pushed the door open and saw a room with two single beds, a dresser, and a book shelf. Although things had changed since David grew up there—the paint, the bedspreads, and a few throw pillows—some things hadn't. Tucked on the shelves were vestiges of David's past. Old

Hardy Boys mysteries, the *Lord of the Rings* trilogy, the *Star Trek* book series—the first *Star Trek*—and even a few college textbooks: *Introduction to Accounting, Fundamentals of Macro Economics* and *Developmental Psychology. Dad took a psychology course?* she thought.

Also on the book shelf were a few tarnished high school baseball trophies and wooden plaques with pictures of the teams on which David played. Meghan picked one up from the 1978-79 school year. She was pretty sure she could pick out her dad amongst the boys on the team. It wasn't too hard. He was the one who looked the most like her. At the bottom of the photo on the brass plate the engraving read Sedona Red Rock High School Scorpions – Division 3A Champs. It was the first time she really connected with the fact that her dad once had a life a lot like hers right now. She chuckled to herself when she spotted, there on the second shelf, a tattered copy of *Go Dog Go*, the much-loved Dr. Seuss classic. Meghan used to have that read to her at pre-school. The similarity of their lives hit home even more, except Dad probably hadn't gone to pre-school, she thought.

As she began to explore more, she found that her dad had excelled as an honor student every report period. She found his old report cards. Ninth grade. Advanced Algebra – A, World Cultures – A, Biology – A, Advanced Composition and Rhetoric – A … Meghan saw for the first time that her dad was a straight-A student. Buried in and amongst the report cards were awards for exceptional academic achievement. Honors from the Sedona post of the American Legion which awarded him a scholarship for college. *I wonder why he never talked about any of this?* she thought.

"I can't believe all this stuff is still here. That you've kept it all. That's so cool," said Meghan. "Dad never told me anything about his high school or his friends or the fact that he was a massive over-achiever. He was a straight A student! Wonder why he never talks about his past."

"I think your dad is a pretty private person. Or maybe he thought you wouldn't be interested. Are kids interested in what their parents were like when they were kids themselves? You know here's something," Ron pulled off the shelf an old star chart that mapped the constellations. "Your dad was very interested in astronomy and space. He wanted to be an astronaut from the time he was a kid until high school. His plan was to go to the moon one day, work for NASA."

"What happened?"

"I don't really know. I was thinking about that not too long ago, actually. It just ended and we never heard him talk about NASA again. It's like his dream vanished," said Ron. "I should ask him sometime."

CHAPTER 18

Not long after Ron and Meghan began exploring, David decided to get in the car and do a little exploring of his own. He wanted to do some thinking about what he was going to do once Meghan graduated next year. Sedona would be a good place to open his thinking. A place away from his normal routine might make him think more clearly.

He decided, while he was thinking, to go in search of a good bottle of wine and some bread for dinner. It seemed like Meghan and his dad were plenty occupied, so he left a note saying he'd be back in a while. Truth was, this was the first chance in a long time that David had to just drive around Sedona, Oak Creek, and Cottonwood. So much had changed. Progress everywhere, businesses plentiful. And beautiful houses tucked into the high desert landscape and red rocks. He was seeing the place with new eyes.

Is Scottsdale where I want to stay? He allowed himself to ask. *It's not like I have a huge network there. Obviously.* Being out of a job had got him thinking. Maybe being out of work was a blessing in disguise. "Let's just drive around a bit and check out the real estate around here.... See what's what," he said to the stop sign on his right.

He turned right and began touring a neighborhood of custom homes within the rolling hills. Every one of them had a view of some red rock monument built by nature. His conclusion after an hour or so? Not much for sale, very pricey, and extraordinarily beautiful. He was marveling at the red rocks, the contrast against the clear blue sky, and the autumn leaves. Picturing himself there, a fresh start, he actually got a small feeling of excitement, a twinge of promise that maybe, just maybe ...

When I was a kid I couldn't wait to leave the small town and all the limitations, he thought. *Is the beautiful scenery getting the best of me? That happens here. In those days, the limitations were real. This place was remote. Today, I guess you can run or be a part of a multinational corporation from a back porch overlooking Bell Rock. And some people do. Living in a small town no longer means a small life.*

David was actually surprising himself with the way he was thinking and feeling. But in classic form he quickly ricocheted back to his comfort zone. As he got back on the main road again, he started peering toward every corner looking for bank branches and wondering if any of them here would want someone from the big city banks in their business loan department. Clearly with the growth of the area, there was a lot more opportunity than there had been when he was a kid. Perhaps thinking Phoenix was the only game in the state was wrong. "Worth thinking about," he said out loud to no one. In the midst of the beautiful sunny day, David felt like he might have a future.

As he sped down route 89A, he glanced to the right. *Oh, man. I haven't driven by this old haunt in forever. We used to try to buy beer here when we were high school kids. We'd usually get kicked out for being under age,* David reminisced as he drove past the old Saddle Spur Bar & Grill outside of Sedona toward Cottonwood. *I have to check this out.* So he pulled a U-turn and slowed down turning right into the small parking lot in the front. Not only did this place bring back memories of high school Friday nights, but also memories of their amazing barbecue and desserts. The place was a local favorite. *Maybe I should bring back something for dessert,* he thought. *And a beer right now sounds pretty good.*

Chapter 18

David walked in the front door and looked around. He was surprised to find there were a few people in the place, still having lunch and mostly watching sports on TV. David sat at the bar and waited for the bartender. "What can I getcha?" the bartender asked.

"Uh, I'll have a Bud Light and then I think I'm going to order some Red Rock Chocolate Cake to go," said David. The bartender nodded and began pouring the beer. Just then, an old voice from the past, boomed louder than the play-by-play commentators on the TVs surrounding the bar. "David? Is that you? Still drinking Bud Light after all these years? I would have thought you moved on to something much more sophisticated by now!" It was Edgar Blackstone, a "kid" from his high school who, well, barely made it through high school. Edgar was always that guy who seemed to make sure everyone knew he was around. He was the opposite of aloof. David could see that his boisterous tendencies had not mellowed with age.

"Hey, Edgar. How are you doing? Yep, still drinking Bud Light." David could sense his afternoon of positive possibilities escaping him with every loud comment made by Edgar. David really wasn't particularly interested in how he was doing.

"Well, I'm doing great, just great. Been living up here since high school, after the military, of course. I spent eight years in the Navy flying helicopters. It was a hoot! No war, powerful aircraft, three squares, and chicks everywhere. I was in San Diego heaven. Plus I was about 40 pounds thinner, so it was pretty great, if you know what I mean."

"I didn't know you entered the Navy after high school," David said, mildly impressed. Edgar didn't seem like he had a lot of smarts in high school. He was always being disruptive in class and spent a portion of every week in detention due to some transgression. It seemed like he couldn't help himself, smoking in the bathrooms, throwing firecrackers down the toilets, and of course, cracking up an entire classroom with one witty, uncensored remark. "And a Navy pilot, to boot. That's really great."

"Yeah, I think the Navy was the only place that could settle me down," Edgar said, but David didn't think he seemed settled down at all. "How about you? What are you up to these days? What are you doing in this dive?"

"Hey, watch it," the bartender/owner remarked, obviously listening to the whole conversation from a short distance away. "This here is a landmark." He was being a little funny, but you could tell his commentary wasn't all jokes. This man had pride of ownership and knew that, in fact, the Saddle Spur was a landmark, written up in travel magazines as a slice of the past in the Southwest. "You are always causing trouble, Edgar," he said, smiling and shaking his head.

"You're right, you're right, amigo. But I'm your best customer—between me and all the people I send here. You have to put up with me. I love you like a brother," he said for all to hear. Then turning to David, "So what's up with you?"

"Oh, not much. You know, the regular stuff. Worked in finance after I got out of college. Then I got married had a daughter, got divorced, you know the usual pathway," David didn't really feel like going into much detail with Edgar. He barely knew him and certainly hadn't hung out with him in school. David was an A-student, college bound. Edgar was a troublemaker. A C-student at best.

"Are you working in Arizona? Do you live in the Valley?" That's what people sometimes call Phoenix, the Valley, which is short for the Valley of the Sun.

"Yeah. Been living in Scottsdale for, gosh, 30 years or so," David felt a moment of pride to say Scottsdale. It does carry with it an air of success and prosperity.

"Ooooh, Scottsdale. You must be rich. Are you rich?" Edgar was never much on finesse. And how crude, David thought, to ask a question like that.

"No, I'm not rich, but I've worked in banking, so I've done okay," boasted David, returning to his old competitive, corporate egotistical ways. This guy banter was actually beginning to make David feel like his old self again. Confident and proud.

"Banking? Commercial or personal?" Edgar asked, suddenly assuming a new intensity. It took David off guard. What would Edgar know about banking?

"Commercial. Why do you ask?" David's curiosity and ego just had to ask. *Commercial sounds so much more impressive,* he thought, *than personal.*

"Well, because you see that truck out there? You see what's written on that truck? Blackstone Adventures. We're the largest outdoor adventure company in Arizona. I started the company 20 years ago after I got fired from every desk job that I got when I left the Navy. I just couldn't stand being cooped up in an office. So I blew off going to college and just took off and started backpacking and rafting, anything I could do to be in the outdoors.

"Pretty soon I got to be an expert with the trails and geology of the area. People started asking me to guide them on hikes, then groups, then corporate groups. It started to get to where I needed to hire people and train them. Today, we have a tour company, with fleets of Hummers and Jeeps. We do overnight trips, day trips, week-long Grand Canyon tours, Colorado river rafting trips. And I've got five birds."

"Birds?" David asked amazed that Edgar owned a company, let alone a successful company without a college education.

"Helicopters, man! We are the biggest air excursion company in the Southwest. We fly the Grand Canyon, Sedona, pretty much anywhere people want to go. Sometime I still do some flying myself. It's a blast." David had heard of Blackstone Adventures. He just never in a million years would have imagined Blackstone meant Edgar. "So the reason I asked about banking is that our business plan this year has us projected to double in size again. And we are on course with our two acquisition targets, one up in Flagstaff and another one up in Page at Lake Powell. We are going to need more birds and boats for the marina. Demand is outstripping supply."

Is this Edgar? Business plans, supply, demand, acquisition targets. David was in shock and thinking to himself, *Am I the only person in the world who bought into the myth of the corporate ladder? Am I the only one who is in my mid-50s and lost? Are you telling me Edgar has his shit together, and I don't?* Thankfully, this time he asked himself these questions silently; it was the first time all day.

"So now that I have a friend in the business—meaning you—what can you do for me in terms of a loan? We've already raised some of the capital from our investors, but we need just a few hundred thousand more. Figure it'd be good to spread my risk."

Investors? Spreading his risk? This was too much for David who instantly didn't feel so Scottsdale grand anymore. "Well Edgar, I'm not really the one that makes loans on businesses like yours but I probably can refer you to a few bankers I know in the industry who could help you." David needed air, he needed to get away. The people he had felt superior to all his life had surpassed him. The C-student out-gunning the A-student.

Then, as if to fire the last bullet dead on target and go for the kill, Edgar blurts out, "Hey, remember Elgin Harris? The brainiac valedictorian of our class?"

"Yeah, of course. What's he up to?" David was thinking NASA jet propulsion engineer.

"He works for me. He's my CFO! Turns out he is a really cool character. He went to Columbia, worked on Wall Street for JP Morgan and got fed up with the rat race of New York. Wanted to come back to the west and didn't need the money. So we partnered up and I gave him a little stake in the company. Turned out to be one hell of a finance guy. He's made us—me—millions!"

David quickly threw his five-dollar bill on the bar for the beer he barely drank and decided to blow off buying the cake for dinner. He had lost his appetite. *Edgar? Really? Ugh! Edgar was least likely to succeed. No college would have ever accepted him. I was number two in the class, behind Elgin, and now look at me!*

Everything David ever believed about getting ahead in life was being shattered. It was as if the universe was assembling one giant lesson plan and he was in the midst of the first semester, having his life turned upside down. He got in the car and began the drive back to Orchard Canyon. He forgot completely about buying the wine and the bread.

Chapter 19

"Hey, Meghan! I found something!" By this time Ron was rooting around under the attic window where his mother's old cedar chest had lived for probably five decades. "Come here. I think you're going to like this." Ron loved the fact that someone in his family was taking an interest in all this old stuff.

"On my way!" Meghan loved exploring, so to her this was nothing short of awesome. First checking out her dad's old room and finding clues to the person he was before he was "Dad," and now, blowing off the dust in the attic and peering back into the 1920s, '30s and '40s in a time machine called Orchard Canyon. What used to seem like ancient history isn't all that distant when you can touch and hold the artifacts of the time, when you can hear people's stories and realize people then weren't all that much different than people are now.

Chapter 19

"Take a look at this," Ron said. In his hands he proudly displayed a photo from the orchard of the late '20s or early '30s. "That's my dad and his brothers at the orchard, working the cider press. That one right there is my dad; those two are his brothers. Look how much smaller the trees are. Some of these original trees are still producing out there today."

"That's the same cider press that's in the Cider Shed now," Meghan stated. "I can't believe that thing is that old."

"Well, save for a few replacement parts we had to fabricate over the years, yep, it's that old."

"This is awesome! This picture will show perfectly how people who lived like my family lived were able to get through the Great Depression. They were able to live on their own. They were like mom, who has a business in fashion but if she had to, she could sew her own clothes. I doubt she will ever have to do that, but still."

"That's correct, Meghan. When you work for yourself and you are a producer. You have an asset like this cider press that produces a product and you have greater control of your future. Of course, my dad and his brothers, me and my brothers, too, we ate a lot of apple everything, drank fresh apple juice. What we didn't use, which was most of the harvest, we sold either as apples or as cider. In good economic times, bad economic times, and the years in between, there was always food on the table from the fruits of that orchard and the juice from that cider press. Not to mention the livestock and the garden."

"Plus, my mother canned, so we had food for the winter. We ate healthy foods compared to today. Look how thin everyone is in this picture. Look at this one of the town. All the people are thin. There was no such thing as fast food or frozen pizza, or TV dinners which became popular when your dad was a kid. That food is terrible for you and will make you fat in a hurry."

Meghan was listening, but still sifting through old photos. "These are perfect. Gramps, you score big points!" Meghan was full of enthusiasm at not just one photo of the orchard and cider making, but six! Including pictures of her family working the old roadside stand, and even Ron's dad at the apple stand that sold the cider magic in glass swing-top bottles.

All Ron could think was, *She called me Gramps* ... and his heart swelled like it hasn't in a very long time.

"Mind if I take these downstairs to show Dad?" Then thinking, "I could just take pictures of them here with my phone I guess," Meghan asked hopeful because first of all, she thought the photos would be easier to take in a place that was brighter; the attic was pretty dark. And second, because she wanted to show her dad how amazing her project and, now, her presentation were going to be!

Ron began gathering up the photos and a few others that might interest David. While putting things back the way he found them, Ron said, "Gramps, huh. I like that. You can call me Gramps, Meghan, whenever you want. You're a good kid."

Meghan felt relieved at last to have a nickname, a name to call her grandfather, "Gramps it is, Gramps!" It came so naturally.

The two made their way down the attic ladder, through the hall and down to the first floor. David had just gotten back from his time in Sedona, returning to the house just in time to be given the chore of heading out to the Apple Shed and fetching a jug of cider from winter storage in the walk-in freezer. The Orchard Canyon Resort always keeps a stock of cider for guests during the late winter. They use it for signature cocktails and culinary delights at The Orchard Canyon restaurant. "No problem, I'll head out there."

He crossed the small parking area and headed into the first barn-like structure known lovingly as the Apple Shed. In it was the cider press, the walk-in freezer, and refrigerator, along with a bunch of worn apple paraphernalia that included more old road signs for the apple stand, like the ones Meghan saw during her barn adventure, old crates and just about anything else you could think of. He walked over to the apple press and took a good look at it. He remembered it as a kid, but never did work the thing. By that time, his dad had a hand who worked alongside him doing the more skilled work like pressing cider. There was no room for error since even then the product was a respected local brand. Quality was paramount. Picking apples, that was another story. *I wonder how many hours this thing is in use putting out cider. How much more could it produce if dad had the apples?* David was well aware that demand was exceeding supply. *Hmmm …*

Knowing dinner was almost ready, David quickly grabbed the jug and headed toward the main house. As they sat down at the table, David noticed Meghan seemed all excited about something. Like she had a surprise to reveal. Then she was about to explode and with a goofy grin on her face, she blurted out. “I saw your baseball trophies and team picture upstairs. Ha! You looked kind of like me, only dorky! Everyone in the picture looked dorky!”

Chapter 19

"Well, it was a dorky time," David said, deadpan, at what was a funny teen comment, but actually quite true. "Let me see that." He took the photo from Meghan. "I was dorky wasn't I? Luckily, I outgrew that phase," he said with a false look of relief.

"Plus, I didn't know you were a brain. You got straight A's. Gramps saved all your report cards. Now I know why I am so obsessed with my grades. It's all YOUR fault!" she said in that teenage, half kidding, half blaming sort of way.

"Well, paaaaaardon me. Caring about how you do in school is a good thing," David said unapologetically. "I will take full credit for your smart genes." Looking at his old report cards brought back memories. "Wow, advanced placement trigonometry, I remember I labored over that class. So theoretical. I guess I was a realist back then, too."

"The other thing we found are these," and she began to fan out the photos of the old cider press, Apple Shed, and stand. "Gramps dug them out of an old cedar box."

"Cedar *chest*, actually, honey," Gramps (Ron) corrected. He wanted her to say it right in her presentation. *And she called me Gramps!* he thought.

"Right, the cedar *chest* up in the attic. And they are perfect for my project and presentation on how people got through The Great Depression. Some went on government work and relief programs, but people like our family from way back had their own businesses that helped them through. I'm finding through my research that people in the cities who worked for companies weren't as stable. Businesses like ours were, and now I have pictures to prove it."

"Lemme see those." David reached across the table, took the one of the cider press in his hand first. He couldn't believe his eyes.

"That's your grandfather and two great uncles," Ron said. But David wasn't looking at the people. He was realizing for the first time that the cider press room he just walked through, that he had been in countless times as a young boy, looked exactly like the picture he was holding. Virtually nothing had changed! Just the people and the clothes.

"My God, the place looks exactly the same, Dad," he spoke his mind.

"Well, not a lot changes around here," said Ron. "I mean of course we have better processes and refrigeration so we can produce more cider. Problem is, I'm getting old and I'm slowing down a little."

"You're hardly slowing down, Dad ..."

"No, I'm slowing down. Not so much doing things around the place, I just don't have the ambition to take on big expansion projects like I used to. Like I did years ago when I added some cabins and started the resort. Plus that keeps us plenty busy. That cider business. It could be big. Maybe when I sell the place, the next owners will take that on ..." Then, without taking a breath, "I'm not planning to sell any time soon, I'll tell you that." Ron looked at Meghan. "You'll have to drag me out of this canyon. You ready!" Ron said with a laugh.

"No way! I don't think I'd be able to get you across the creek," said Meghan, now laughing, thinking how funny it would look, her grandfather kicking and screaming as she tried to get him across the creek that flows over the drive into the resort. That would be quite a scene.

David started thinking about apple cider. "Hey, I brought the cider in, got it warming on the stove and we haven't even had any yet. I'll go get it." David walked to the cupboard and grabbed a few mugs. He ladled the warm cider and carried two mugs to the table, then his own, and sat back down. He couldn't help but think, as he took that first sip, that his father was right. The cider business could be much bigger than it was.

The hour spent with Edgar was demoralizing, but also inspiring. *If Edgar could do something on his own and be successful, why couldn't I,* David thought. Edgar didn't even go to college. He just started doing something he loved, knew how to do and it became a business. No one in the corporate world thinks that way. *Maybe this is the wake up call I needed. That cider press is intriguing. Step one might be helping Dad get some financing.*

Chapter 19

CHAPTER 20

David tossed in his bed, fitful and wide awake that night with thoughts spinning in his head. For the first time in weeks that worthless feeling he had since being shown the door at the bank left him when he was at his Dad's house. He saw a tiny light at the end of the tunnel. *Maybe this is the change I need.*

All during dinner, Ron told stories about working the cider press as a kid. How much they used to produce and how they kept making more and more as the trees produced even more apples and they acquired more orchard land. People love the stuff and even today it sells out in stores around Arizona in a matter of hours. Early in his career when he handled small business loans, David became very good at spotting ideas that could work from those that were a long long shot.

Chapter 20

He couldn't stop thinking, *Yes, there is life beyond working for a bank. The cider business ... that could be something*—his thoughts trying to convince him. That's how his little chat with himself started out. But then his inner voice turned on him, as it often did whenever he treaded a little too far from its comfort zone.

What do you know about running a business? A cider business? Are you kidding me? You pushed paper for a living at a bank. Now the paper is going away, you've been replaced by a computer portal. Running a cider business ... are you crazy? How would you afford it? That was his inner voice killing his glimmer of hope. Inner voices often do that if you let them and at this moment, David was defenseless.

His negative thoughts got big, bigger still because it was 3:18 am and he was all alone in his big house as he is most nights unless Meghan was there. *What am I thinking? I can't just pick up and hide in the cider shed, in that canyon ... I thought I had life pretty figured out. I had a good job; I felt secure. That paycheck. What I'd do now to even have half of that salary coming in every two weeks. What can I* do? *What will I do?*

This was the first time in David's life that he truly realized how vulnerable he had been. He was in no position to be thankful that his life had been pretty easy up until now. *What if this had happened when Meghan was just a baby? Who cares! It's happening now. She wants to go to college. Where is that money going to come from? I'm not asking Susan to pay for college, any of it. She can afford it, obviously. That's the sad part. But God, I'd feel like a loser. I do feel like a loser. Loser.*

This little voice conversation with himself was getting him nowhere except further into the depths of his own depression. *What about moving up to Sedona?*

Then came that voice again. *You can't do that. How would you sell your house? Your mortgage and your second mortgage—you know, the one you took out because you just had to have that $100,000 kitchen remodel. You're upside down; you owe more than this house is worth. Real estate values are climbing, but they are not what they used to be. Sell your house, Einstein, and you'd owe money. You're a banker; you know that.*

I feel trapped.

You are trapped. You're going to have to downsize.

Downsize. I hate the word "downsize." I feel like a failure.

Chapter 20

You are a failure, David. You have no house, really, because the bank owns the roof over your head. And you have no one. No one who cares enough about you to help you out of this mess. You tried. You called people you know, and nothing.

You're right. I do have no one. How does a person go through 57 years on this earth and have no real relationships. I'm an idiot. My relationships have been with my computer at the office, my chair, the TV when I got home, and the stuff I just had to have.

Maybe you need to find some wealthy woman to take care of you.

Shut up. I don't need anybody. I don't need anyone.... His thoughts trailed off. That was really it. He always felt he didn't need anyone and until now he didn't. He had bought into the rhetoric of go to school, get a degree, get a good job, claw your way to the top and take as much as you could to win. Well what happens when you don't get to the top? The place where the big decisions happen. Decisions like who is merging with who, what the next acquisition will be, and who stays and who goes.

I'll answer that. You become a sitting duck. Even though you don't feel like a sitting duck. You're enjoying the scenery, grabbing a few fish too small for the big guys and loving it. Thinking all the while that you got this big lake, blue sky, and endless sunny days just like this one, ahead of you. It's an illusion. That's your view.

Yeah, the other view is through life's cross-hairs. I guess it was just a matter of time before the trigger got pulled and the illusion vanished. Sad part is, I didn't even appreciate it while I was in it. How much energy I wasted being angry at the small stuff. Faucets dripping, a ding in a car door, Susan nagging me about getting home for dinner.

You should have eaten more dinners at home.

Yeah, easy to say now. But there were deals to analyze, reports to run, and presentation "decks" to create. Presentation decks, what a waste of time developing a bunch of slides that bored a room to tears. I chose that over doing something I enjoyed—I hated putting those damn things together—yet I clicked and typed my way along from morning until night.

Working to create more wealth for the people who cut you off at the knees. They cut you off at the knees. David had had enough. He couldn't lie here any longer shifting from side to side trying his best to escape his reality.

I am option-less. I have nowhere to go. What are my options? Where am I financially? I don't even know. I'm afraid to look.

Get up and look. Maybe it's not as bad as you think. But I wouldn't count on it.

I need to get up and put some numbers down. I have to get a handle on what's going on in my life.

You may want to make a list of stuff you can sell.

Stop it.

David threw off the covers that betrayed him and threw his pillow aside. His bed was not a place of rest. His mobile phone lit his path as he made his way into the kitchen. Dishes were left on the counter from a day or so ago. He decided to put those away, finally. He noticed a few spots on the counter and decided it was a good time to clean that mess up. *Coffee ... I need some coffee.* He poured himself a cup of yesterday's brew that was still in the pot and warmed it in the microwave.

Avoidance, you're avoiding the truth, his inner voice told him. *Sit down and face your reality.*

This time his inner voice was right, so he sat down at his desk and began looking at how he could possibly make the changes he knew he must make in his life. He started to ask himself the hard questions about what those changes might be.

CHAPTER 21

Meghan tossed and turned in her bed at Susan's house, too. It was that time of year, her senior year in high school, when all students who had dreams of college were sweating acceptance letters for the college of their choice. Meghan, although a good student, had her concerns, just like most of her friends had. Her college dream was UCLA and she knew the level of competition she was up against. Kids with better grades, more community service, in-state residency. *What if I don't get in?* she worried most of the night.

Meghan was excited about going to college. But a lot of her friends were not like her. They were "expected" to go to college. It was just the next thing. Many didn't really believe it was needed to get ahead in life. *That works for some people* she thought, *but you have to know what else you're going to do if you're not going to college*. And most of her friends who were not enthusiastic about college, didn't really have any plan. They just didn't want to go.

One of Meghan's friends, Grayson Garrett, however, did have a plan. He had been a computer geek developing software programs from the time he was a kid. Technically he wasn't a geek, he was a nerd, and not in a good way. Being a geeky, nerd is kind of cool, but not to this level. He was awkward in so many ways, but brilliant. And super smart. In fact, he had developed a technology platform at the ripe age of 15 that last year was purchased by a large tech company to integrate into their online platform. He had a ton of money and he was only 17.

He also knew how to use the Internet to learn everything he needed to learn. "It's all there," he said recently when Meghan was paired with him for a chemistry project. Grayson knew how to source information, any information. It didn't matter how obscure. Online learning was natural for him and he went to high school because he had to. He was well beyond that having taken electrical engineering courses from Penn State, technical writing from MIT, business law classes from Harvard and a 400-level course on game theory from Stanford. He also listened to their Entrepreneurial podcast series for fun.

"For fun!" Meghan exclaimed while lying in her bed scrolling through pictures of the "Best Dressed Celebs at a charity gala" feature online. *This is fun,* she thought.

He practically had a college degree without ever stepping foot on a campus. In fact, he took his placement tests for Arizona State University and discovered he could get both his undergraduate and graduate degrees in about two years total. He was that advanced. "Maybe when I get time," he said when Meghan asked him about his college plans. "I don't really need it and I have an app that is in final development that will be ready to launch next fall, so I'll be busy."

Grayson impressed Meghan, but she also wondered what his parents were like. "Dad would freak out if I said I wanted to skip college—no matter how many apps I had in development. Even if I said I wanted to work in Mom's business and blow off college, Dad would say, 'Absolutely not. You get nowhere without a college degree.' Grayson's parents must be okay with it." Truth was, Grayson's parents weren't just okay with it, they were invested in his next brilliant venture and securing capital from outside investors. Grayson's mom had technical acumen herself and, after years of experience in technology, was part of a venture capital firm that funded start-ups. His dad was a successful engineer with a number of patents.

That was Grayson. Meghan wanted to go to UCLA, she dreamed about it ever since she visited her cousin there a year ago. The anticipation was killing her. She couldn't sleep. To add to the drama, some of her friends had already received acceptance letters. Screams were echoing in her high school hallways, "OMG! I got accepted there too! We can be roommates!"

Maybe they send out all the acceptance letters first and then they send out the rejection letters after all the slots are filled. What if that's how it works? Maybe that's why I haven't heard anything from any of the schools I applied to? Maybe I'll have to work for Mom's company. Maybe Grayson can use some help …

Sleep wasn't going to happen for Meghan, so she got up to find her iPad and check out what was going on with her favorite YouTubers sharing the funny, the gross, and the insane with her friends on Instagram. If nothing else she could shock her friends first thing in the morning. That has to count for something.

CHAPTER 22

The dawn's first light brought a gray glow to David's office. When he sat down an hour before, the room had been completely dark, except for the glow of the computer screen. It was symbolic of his gray reality: that he was screwed financially. "How could I have let this happen?" he said, beating himself up and no longer needing his inner voice to do the lashing. "I'm in banking, for God sake! I paid attention to everyone else's money and future and completely blew off my own. No wonder Susan left me. I took care of everyone else except her... and Meghan."

That last thought pierced him through the heart. He hadn't taken care of his own child. And while David may have been, due to his lack of sleep, a little too hard on himself, this was his reality. He was thankful to be alone with his anger and remorse.

I have stuff. Not smarts. I have a BMW (had to have it) that I owe more on than it is worth. I have a house (had to have that, too) that I owe more on than it is worth. The first home equity loan for the kitchen remodel (had to have it). That second home equity loan for the boat (had to have it). It has to have an inch of dust on it at the boat storage. Never use it. With my financial picture, I can't afford the gas to power it! What was I thinking? I guess I wasn't thinking. I never thought anything would go wrong.

His largest asset was a Schwab 401(k) that had about $400,000, which he couldn't touch without a stiff penalty, so said the financial advisor. *I got sucked into the lure of the corporate matching, the benefits—golden handcuffs. I should have followed my gut at the first merger and made the leap after Susan did. I thought of leaving fifteen years ago. But the incentive trips, and I was so close to my bonus that year, and the following year they increased our stock options.... I always had a reason to stay.*

That morning, he began opening his statements, the ones he had thrown in his desk drawer unopened. When the recession hit in 2008, he lost a lot of his portfolio value, as did almost everyone else. Sometime in 2009, he stopped opening the envelopes, and they just kept piling up quarter by quarter. *I may as well see it all*, he thought on this dark morning. Statement by statement he saw how his portfolio had fallen and then risen. He was optimistic as he stacked the statements in order. *Maybe I have more in here than I thought.* But then reality hit. Even though the markets had regained most if not all the losses during the recession, his particular portfolio had not done as well as he had hoped. "I'm paying fees for a fund that is underperforming the S&P? Which I could invest in for free!" His heart sank.

If this little exercise did one thing, it helped David to realize that he was not alone. He had plenty of friends who had all their eggs in one basket and were in the same predicament. They had the same single stream of income, the same 401(k) and the same if not more toys. *I always had to keep up. Why? Well, now I'm paying the price. I could sell it all and, to get out of debt, owe practically my entire retirement just to break even. And soon I'll have no income. My severance is running out. If I was a client of mine, I'd recommend filing for chapter 11 bankruptcy.*

That reality hit David hard. Why didn't he make himself his own client? He had great common sense with everyone else, but himself? It was all ego. *That's what it was. I had to show I was better than everyone else. Well, now I'm just like everyone else. Living on the edge of collapse. One lost job, one medical problem, one catastrophe—and not even a big one—from financial ruin.*

The fire was lit yet again. *I have to find a banking job. Maybe I'll find one out of state, that way the company will relocate me and buy my house—that would take care of that problem. California would be good. Meghan wants to go to college at UCLA anyway.* At that moment, David got a sinking feeling in the pit of his stomach. *College. How am I going to pay for Meghan's college?*

At this point the gray light of early dawn had transformed into the gray light of a rare cloudy day in Scottsdale. *Perfectly fitting,* he thought as he looked out the window. *There is no blue sky in any of this.*

His distraction didn't last long. He pulled up a new browser window and typed in Southern-California-bank-executive jobs. Up popped a job site that had 237 bank executive jobs in Southern California. About 4,000 management jobs. He clicked on the first one he came to: Branch manager. *Ugh. The thought of dealing with the minutia of running a branch again,* he thought.

The listing clearly stated, "Candidates should be advised that City National Bank does not pay interviewee travel expenses or relocation expenses for candidates who are hired unless previously agreed."

I can't afford to take a job like this. I am trapped! I am literally trapped. Executive jobs have to pay for relocation. I mean, you'd think ... his voice trailed off as he scrolled down to find a position opening as a wholesale account executive selling mortgage products in California and Texas. *But the company's based in Florida. Extensive travel... I could just spend a lot of time in California. Salary $100,000 to $200,000. The high end is close to what I was making... Oh, it's commission sales. Forget it.*

He kept scanning. JPMorganChase Relationship Manager. That sounds more like it, working with business clients and securing new accounts. In Los Angeles. No salary listed... David quickly pulled up another browser window and checked on the salary range for a position like this in LA. *Fifty-six thousand dollars to $71,000! Who can live in Los Angeles for that?*

After about an hour more of California listings, David abandoned his hope for a paid move to LA and also came to realize the kind of executive position he had was virtually non-existent in the second biggest city in the nation. So he broadened his search. While he was scrolling through the countless sales jobs, he noticed one that was all too telling. It was Deloitte looking for bank transformation experts. That said it all. The banking industry was transforming. He kept scrolling working hard to see a glimmer that would indicate his role in business had not become obsolete. *I'm only 57 and I'm a dinosaur.* He started to come to terms with reality.

With the realization that he was going nowhere, that he was wasting his time looking online for jobs, he thought *Can you imagine what the competition must be like in L.A.? Why would they relocate me when there are plenty of people in L.A. the bank can hire? People who aren't dinosaurs.* Meghan's college popped back into his mind. *What am I going to do? What am I going to do?* He shook his head and leaned into his hands, elbows on the burl wood desk (had to have it). Tears fell on the blotter covering the expensive desk he still did not fully own.

It had been clear for many years. David just refused to believe it. Online banking has replaced and would continue to replace a lot of the work he used to do. Automation in banking was all around him and his ego kept telling him, "You can't be replaced. The work you do is important." It was important. So important, in fact, that creating digital platforms that work 24/7 and don't ask for raises, that don't take vacation, never stay home on sick days, and don't require bonuses suddenly made perfect sense. David began to realize his days in banking were done.

That led him to the realization that, in his current state of mind, he had no other skills. *What else can I do? Banking is all I know. Everyone said, "Get good at something. Become an expert." So I became an expert.* "No one told me what would happen if that thing I became an expert in ceased to exist. What about that?" He was shouting now, angry, feeling as if he had been duped by the world. He had taken the word as law, built his entire life inside a true house of cards. And now the bottom card had been pulled out. Part of the house had collapsed with the rest of it teetering perilously.

What am I going to do ...

Chapter 23

CHAPTER 23

David and Meghan arrived at Orchard Canyon by mid-morning the following Sunday. Both had been quiet on the drive up. Meghan was tuned into her headphones, whatever she was listening to, and David was just lost in his own thoughts. Both had worries they didn't want to share with the other. Neither of them bothered to ask the other what was wrong. They didn't care, and were happy not to have to respond. It was a perfect symbiosis.

But when the Beemer pulled into the resort and drove up to the main house, Ron was just finishing up a conversation with a neighbor and fellow hospitality colleague, Marian Ritter, who owned the small motel up the road. She was a lovely woman, slender, in her late 70s, with thick shoulder-length silver hair. Ron held in his hand a casserole dish that Marian had brought to him. They had known each other for decades and Marian knew Ron loved Italian food so she had made him a dish of lasagna. “Stay here a minute, would you? That way you could say hello to David and my granddaughter. You haven’t seen my son in ages and I’m not sure you ever met Meghan.”

“She was just a baby, if I recall.”

“She’s 17 now!”

“Oh, that makes me feel a lot older! There they are. She is lovely!”

“David, Meghan, hurry on over and meet my friend Marian.”

David quickened his pace out of respect, but was dreading every minute of seeing Mrs. Ritter. Again, all that awkwardness of answering questions. He decided to take the offensive and ask her questions before she could ask him about work and family, and “the update.” That sounded like a winning strategy.

“David, you remember Mrs. Ritter, right?

“Of course. How are you, Mrs. Ritter? This is my daughter, Meghan.”

“So nice to see you, David.” Mrs. Ritter’s eyes were smiling and her face lit up. “Meghan, you were an infant last time I saw you. Can’t believe it because here you are all grown up.”

"Hi," Meghan said, knowing the adults were going to continue their conversation. And she really didn't want the college question to come up. She might just break down and cry if asked where she was going come September.

David and Meghan stopped on the porch mostly because Ron and Mrs. Ritter were blocking the door that led to the living room. They began sharing how nice it was to live near each other so they could look out for each other and get together. That's what community is.

"That and lasagna," said Ron with a smile and his hands now holding this prize feast, courtesy of neighborly generosity and caring.

Rather than wait to be asked "How are you doing?" David decided to ask Mrs. Ritter how she'd been and what was the occasion for the lasagna.

"Oh, you know, not really an occasion, just happy to bring your dad a little something. Heaven knows he supplies me with the best apples year after year." David, rather than being a cynic, realized that this kind of neighborly sharing was completely foreign to him. He had spent his whole life competing *against* people, not helping them. Every morning he woke up and spent his day clawing to the top. That was the corporate reality. If you win, it means others have to lose. But here in this magical canyon were two people, who both owned resorts on the same scenic route 89A, and they were not competitors, but friends who talked with each other and shared apples, lasagna, and life.

When David got home from the battlefield known as work, he drove directly into the garage and closed the door. Neighbors were non-existent. Friendly hellos never happened. David's neighbors pulled into their garages and closed their doors, too. Many fought on their own corporate battlefields and were as tired as he was.

David walked back to the car to unload a few things, including a bottle of wine. He thought he might need it later in the day. As he was opening the back door, he thought to himself that in his life, friends, real friends, were non-existent; David had only colleagues. And given the way he treated them at the office, the way they treated each other, they were always on guard. No wonder no one wanted to help him in this struggle. He lived in an "every man for himself" world, a far cry from the community in this canyon, even in the bigger town of Sedona.

"Why don't you come back this evening and enjoy a pot roast with us, Marian? I have one ready to go. The kids are staying and it will be a nice chance to get caught up after, what, 17 years. Can it really be that long since you've seen them?"

"I don't want to impose..."

"No imposition. Really, we'd love to have you join us."

"Okay, then. Yes. I would love to stop by. What time?"

"Let's say three o'clock."

"Three it is!" Marian smiled and gave an affirming nod as she turned and walked toward her truck. David was walking toward the porch with the bags from the car in his arms. "See you later today. I'm looking forward to getting all caught up on the life of David!"

"Great, see you then." A pain in the pit of his stomach hit him hard and, at that point, David could not have been more thankful. His decision to bring the wine was nothing short of divine inspiration.

Throughout the day, Meghan worked on her senior project and presentation, gathering up more artifacts from the barn and the attic. In one box she found an old picture of some family ancestor, not sure who, in front of the first school in Sedona, Red Rock School. That got her thinking about what school must have been like during the Depression. Were kids still able to go or did they have to help the family make ends meet? She started to channel her nerdy friend Grayson and research schools during the Great Depression. *He's right, everything is online.*

What she learned was kind of surprising because you'd think public schools were founded by the government. But in article after article about the history of public schools, she found that it was wealthy industrialists who influenced the curriculum more than anyone else. They donated a lot of money to create the schools the way they wanted them. She had to look up what an industrialist was and found it was a person who owned an industrial business and often made a lot of money from that business. Guys like Nelson Rockefeller, J. Paul Getty, and Andrew Carnegie were wealthy industrialists. She found articles that showed the schools in those days taught students what was needed to work in these industrialists' plants, refineries, and steel mills. They were training people for the work of the day.

That's so interesting, Meghan thought, because at her school, which was rather progressive, she was learning how to produce videos and develop websites. *Just like way back when, that stuff is preparing me for the real world we live in*, Meghan thought. One article, however, was disturbing because it said that some current school systems have not evolved enough. That what schools are teaching will be obsolete before students can ever use it in the real world. The workforce is becoming more mobile and autonomous, yet schools are still teaching as if we will all be corporate employees.

Meghan thought about that while she rummaged through some of the other finds she had dispersed around her. *I so hope I get into UCLA. I want to do something in film or fashion, and that would be soooo perfect! God, if you let me get accepted to UCLA, I promise I will never roll my eyes at Dad again. I promise I won't say one swear word ever again.* As she was hoping and praying and promising, she thought about Grayson. *Maybe he had it right. I still absolutely want to go to UCLA, but maybe expecting school to be the only place where I learn the stuff I need to know is wrong. Maybe I should be spending more time online preparing for my future rather than keeping up with the celeb gossip. Okay, not rather than. Let's say in addition to,* she made that compromise with herself.

While Meghan was seeing the reality of modern-day learning and the importance of self-enrichment, David was coming to grips with his own reality: that he was going to have to come clean and tell his dad what was going on in his life. The two of them were in the apple shed doing a little heavy lifting. Barrels, harvesting bins, and equipment needed to be moved from one end of the building to the other. "C'mon, Dad. I'll give you a hand with those." Ron had mentioned he had intended to get that done, but then Marian stopped over.

"Let's just move these," he said, pointing to the bins in the cider press room, "over to there," looking in the direction of the apple washing area and the door closest to the orchard. "I keep them there in the off season so they are out of the way but close by when we need them. August will be here before you know it."

August, then September, then college for Meghan, David's inner voice was talking loudly during this rare manual labor.

"David, you're panting like a 90-year-old," Ron joked. "I'd say 80-year-old, but you're breathing harder than me!"

"I guess I'm a little bit out of shape. It's hard to find the time to exercise with work and everything," David spoke those words reflexively, he'd said them so many times to friends, Susan, himself, now his dad. The trouble was that, this time, it occurred to him, there was no "work" to use as an excuse. He had all the time in the world.

"Well, you have to just tell those people at the bank that you need a little time for yourself. Or you're going to find yourself in the hospital. And you'll be no good to them there." Ron made perfect sense, but nonsense in the realities of the corporate world. A lot of managers talk a good game of work-life balance, but don't like when you actually try to achieve it. You go nowhere and the guy or gal who burns the midnight oil gets the promotion.

"If only it worked that way, Dad."

"Well, you're senior enough by now to take a little time for yourself, right? To get home in time to make a meal and eat better, to get out and exercise. Those aren't chores, David. They are among the pleasures of life."

"I know, Dad. You're right. Those things matter." David wasn't just agreeing. He knew his dad was showing his concern. David was concerned about his health, too. All the stuff he would hear about GMO foods, the obesity crisis, and all the illnesses that come from a sedentary life. He was playing right into all of them. He was one of the 30 percent of Americans who were obese. He was a massive consumer of processed food. All genetically modified. He never just went for a walk. He never worked up a sweat. What happened to him? It's like he stopped caring about himself in the race for the top.

"What's wealth without health?" Ron interrupted. "I know you do well financially. I just want to make sure you're around to enjoy it. I don't want to see you get sick. You're too young for that, but only if you take care of yourself. Otherwise you're the perfect age for the onset of illness. Diabetes, heart attacks—there's too much of that because people eat too much crap and don't move enough. Come up here more and me and the guys who help me with this place will keep you moving and eating right," Ron said, meaning every word of it. He'd love to have his son at Orchard Canyon more often.

"I hear you," David said. He was getting bombarded by two people in the room. His dad and his inner voice.

When are you going to tell him, David? his inner voice hostile now. *You're such a coward. This is your chance. It's just the two of you. How are you going to answer his question? Another lie? Change the subject? C'mon, coward, be a man.*

"Dad, the truth is..."

"David, over here. Can you grab that side of the feed bag and on three, we'll pick it up and bring it to the chicken coop." Ron interrupted David, in the hope that they could carry a 50-pound bag of chicken feed about 75 yards to the hen house. "On three...

one... two... three," they picked up the bag and began walking out the door. "This is so much easier with your help. Nice having you around here, son." Then as if it were an afterthought, "You were saying?"

"Oh, nothing. I don't remember. Must not have been very important." The moment had passed, along with David's courage.

You got a temporary pass, his inner voice said.

Chapter 24

CHAPTER 24

"Why is Mom calling me? Hello?"

"Hi, honey! Where are you, are you at your Dad's?"

"No, we're up at Gramps' house. I'm working on my senior project. Just found some amazing stuff. A picture of the first school in Sedona. It looked like a shack. Big difference between that and Chaparral High School where I go. There's like a hundred rooms there, and this was a school with one tiny room. I also have come to the realization that school may not be preparing me for my future."

"Really, now. How did you arrive at that?" Susan was curious, because she couldn't help but feel the same. The world was moving so fast, with new technologies introduced continually, that schools couldn't possibly keep up. The best they could do is teach what they can and most importantly, teach kids how to continue to learn.

"Well, I read an article about how schools aren't keeping pace with the realities of a more autonomous workforce." Meghan used the exact words in the article.

Susan asked, "Do you know what they mean by that?"

"Kind of. I think it means that people want to do their own thing. Kind of like Grayson is doing his software development," Meghan answered, a little unsure of herself.

"That's quite true. It also means that more and more people are going to work for themselves because they are finding they can't count on their employers. There's no loyalty there anymore, so there's a push toward independent contracting, where people work for themselves. A lot of our employees are really contractors." Susan thought this was a good opportunity to impart some business knowledge, even though that was not why she had called.

"Yeah, I'm seeing through Dad that you can't count on ..." Meghan stopped herself. She almost blew it! *Stop talking,* she thought.

"Seeing what through Dad?" Susan wanted her to finish her thought.

"Oh, just that business is business. He always says that." Meghan made a veiled attempt to be vague. But Susan's "Meghan radar" as well as her "David radar" was up. Something was going on.

"Well, the reason I called is to tell you there are some letters here ...."

"Letters?" Meghan had no idea what her mother was getting at.

"Letters, you know, letters ... from colleges ..." Susan was being a little playful with the whole matter.

"Well, open them!!!!" Meghan shouted.

"No, that's not how it works. Tomorrow when you are back after school, we'll sit down and open them together. This is an important moment in your life—good or bad—and it shouldn't happen over the phone. One way or another your future will happen and it will be the right one for you."

"I can't believe you won't open the letters. Is one from UCLA?"

Chapter 24

"I'm going to hang up now—be happy —you are on your way!" Susan wanted to build the suspense. She had no doubt her exceptional daughter would be accepted to just about anywhere.

"This is why mothers drive their daughters crazy," Meghan said out loud as the phone call ended.

Meghan tried to return to her project, but her concentration was non-existent. She was filled with suspense and dread at the same time. She texted her mother, "Can't you just please open the letters?" and got in return both a smiley emoji and a kiss face emoji. *I guess that's a loving "no,"* Meghan thought.

She got online and typed in UCLA.edu. She couldn't help just wanting to know if she got in. By checking out the admissions page and the housing page and the curriculum pages, she felt closer to her dream. Or what she hoped would be the realization of her dream. There'd be no getting back to her senior project today.

She bundled up all the original photos and decided she'd do one last task of organizing the digital files into the PowerPoint. She dreamed about how this could one day be a documentary. A story about her own family and the way they made it through one of the toughest times in American history. *There's a lesson in this* she thought. *Gramps' story is about self-sufficiency, surrounded by family and friends. So is Mom's, come to think about it.*

Text: "Open the letters!!!!!!"

Text back: "Nope!" and a heart emoji.

Chapter 25

Chapter 25

Smells like pot roast, Meghan thought as she made her way downstairs from her ongoing escapades in the attic and her online tour of the UCLA website. The place was home to so many artifacts from the past, and here it was already well past one o'clock. She had been so engrossed in her project that she hadn't given any thought to lunch. "Dad? Gramps?" Meghan wondered where everyone was. Then she caught sight of them outside repairing one of the 100-year-old doors on Cabin 10.

One of the doors had gotten stuck, and while they were at it, the door's hinges needed to be oiled. "May as well oil them all," Ron said, "Particularly since I have a partner." David was glad to be needed and productive; it was a good diversion from reality and it was nice to be doing something physical. Particularly after the discussion about health an hour earlier. *Dad's right and no point in denying it. Get moving, David,* he thought.

Just about that time, Meghan could hear Mrs. Ritter's truck driving across Oak Creek and up the narrow drive to the property. Marian waved to Ron and David as she parked in the lot. Meghan could just barely hear, "I thought I'd come a bit early in case you needed any help with dinner."

"Just make yourself at home at the house, we'll be done here in a little while. If you really want to help, I have some salad fixings in the sink—a cucumber, some celery and carrots—that you could chop up if you don't mind," Ron said.

"Of course, I'm happy to help. Keeping busy means staying young!" Marian walked over to the house and spotted Meghan. "Well, good afternoon to you, young lady!"

"Hi, Mrs. Ritter," Meghan didn't really know what more to say. She didn't remember her. Luckily, Mrs. Ritter took the lead and was as friendly as she could be.

"Hi, Meghan, I just got my kitchen assignment from your grandfather. Want to help?" this seemed like the perfect time, the perfect opportunity to get to know Meghan a bit better. After all, this is a close-knit community here and she should know Ron's grandchildren, all of them.

"Sure, okay. What do you want me to do?" Meghan put her phone down on the table.

"First, wash your hands and grab some dishes from the cupboard, some silverware to set the table, that would be a big help. The boys look like they have had a day of repairs and chores. What have you been up to?" Marian knew the best way to get a teenager talking was to have her talk about herself.

"I was working on my senior project. It's about how people survived during the Great Depression. I mean work-wise, and even school." Meghan realized how hard it was to encapsulate all that she had discovered into one sentence.

"What did you find out?" Marian was truly interested in this topic. Her parents had been in their early 20s when the U.S. economy collapsed. She had heard bits and pieces from them when she was growing up.

"Gramps has been really helpful. In addition to my research on how people got through that scary time, he's told me stories about when he was growing up and how his parents were always worried there'd be another Depression. They never fully trusted the banks again, he said."

Chapter 25

"My parents told me stories like that too," said Mrs. Ritter. "I was a little girl when those hard times hit."

"Were you living in Sedona?" Meghan asked.

"Oh, no, dear. No, no. my family was from Brooklyn. There was no work for my father so my parents took what little they had and moved west. My dad was lucky enough to get a public works job building the Hoover Dam. It was dangerous work, but it was work. Of course, it was called Boulder Dam when he was working on it," Mrs. Ritter said.

"Wow! That must have been a big change coming from Brooklyn and going to Nevada," Meghan said with astonishment. She had only seen Hoover Dam once and even today there's not much around it. "Where did you live?"

"When I think of my parents packing up and moving with my my older brothers and sisters, I can hardly believe. There were five of them. Then I came along last once they were out west. I was born in Boulder City, Nevada, which was a housing settlement for families working on the dam. It wasn't very posh, if I remember correctly," she said with a chuckle. "But, you know, I think everyone did what they had to do in those days," her voice trailed off as she gazed out the window above the sink.

"Sounds like your family didn't want to leave Brooklyn," Meghan could be pretty perceptive when she wanted to be, and she was getting comfortable with Mrs. Ritter. She was a nice woman.

"You're right. They didn't want to leave. I mean, imagine all the relatives were there. And my brothers and sisters, a few of them were in school and had friends. To pick up and leave for the middle of nowhere ... There was no choice. It was either that or the bread lines. It was survival. And there were no cell phones or text messages, right? So when you left, you left. Letter writing, that's how people stayed in touch." Mrs. Ritter laughed, trying to lighten the mood. It truly was hard for her family to completely leave civilization for the Wild West. "We'd only see my father on some weekends. His work crew was far away from the small houses we were all living in outside of Las Vegas. There were hardly any people living there before the dam, but then the town grew to about 20,000 people, many hoping to find work as day laborers doing anything to make money."

"Mind if I use your story in my report about how people got through the Depression? That's a really good one. So far I have my Gramps' story of being pretty much self-sufficient in this canyon. And now yours of having to go clear across the country to get a job." Meghan recapped Mrs. Ritter's words.

Chapter 25

"Add to that, Meghan, that my dad was a banker in Brooklyn. He was a professional man. But with so many banks, including his, that shut down, there were no jobs for people like him, so he did what many others did, took a job doing manual labor, whatever he could get. Gosh, looking back, though, Hoover Dam ..." Mrs. Ritter stared out the window as she washed the celery in the sink. "Look what he has to show for his efforts. He was more proud of that while he was alive than he ever was about his banking work. He never talked about any of that. But he used to love to talk about the dam!"

"So it was a good experience, then?" asked Meghan.

"It really was, working with his hands and building something from nothing. Something monumental. It was life-changing. To me, I was just a kid and didn't know anything else. Nevada was an adventure and I made lots of friends. I did things I never would have done had we stayed in Brooklyn."

"Like what?"

"I learned to ride horses, and rope. We had chickens so I'd feed them and gather up the eggs every day. All the stuff a rural life in the West is famous for. It was a lot more fun for me growing up in Nevada than it would have been in Brooklyn I have to believe," said Mrs. Ritter

"How did you get to Arizona and Oak Creek Canyon?" Meghan asked .

"Eventually, as things improved and my parents were able to save some of what my father earned—he continued to work for the dam, eventually in management—they took what money they had and bought a little property up the road in this canyon. Like your family, it was a place to live, grow food, and even rent out a space or two to people passing through. It wasn't a hotel back then, but it was the first time I think my parents ever felt secure."

"That seems to be a pattern, I'm learning. Security comes through being self-sufficient rather than depending on a company for a job." Meghan was starting to see the truth, understanding more and more why her own dad was suffering his own Great Depression.

Dinner was almost ready and it would be just a few more minutes before Ron and David made their way back to the main house. "Let's chop up these vegetables for the salad to make sure we have everything ready for when the boys get back in. They are going to be hungry, I bet."

Chapter 26

CHAPTER 26

With all the bins in their rightful places and not one, but three heavy bags of chicken feed moved to the hen house, and 10 doors oiled, David was really winded and ready for a break. And somehow Ron, 35 years David's senior, was barely phased.

They sat down on one of the cabin porches overlooking Oak Creek, "Not to harp on this, son, but when was the last time you took care of yourself? I mean, like most parents you do everything for your kids, but you are getting to the age where you have to start paying attention to yourself."

David wasn't really in the mood to get into this again. Susan used to be good enough at that rhetoric and gave him enough of it for a lifetime. "I get it, Dad. I just get busy and can't find the time to exercise. Then I'm in a hurry, I'm hungry and well, McDonald's is right there," David said, thinking *why make excuses?* "Then there's all that rich food at client dinners. That's how it works. That's how you get to be 57, overweight, and out of shape."

"I don't mean to upset you, David. I'm just worried, that's all." Ron felt he may have pushed a little too hard.

"No, Dad, it's not you. You're right about all that. I have to change my ways, starting today. About a lot of things. I've been meaning to tell you. It's just been hard," David stalled.

"What is it, son? Are you not well?" Ron was visibly worried.

"No, no it's nothing like that. You see about two months ago, I got laid off from the bank. A reorganization after a damn merger *I* helped orchestrate. How do you like that? And since then, I not only haven't found work. I feel ... I feel ... lost. For the first time in my life, I don't know what my next step should be." David felt like a weight had been lifted, finally, by coming clean. Then he felt like a failure in the eyes of his dad. A disappointment. At this age, having job problems. It was like a midlife crisis for someone planning to live to 114.

"Well, I'm glad to hear that. Not that you're out of work, but that you're not sick. The way you started talking, my stomach did a somersault," Ron said, clearly relieved.

"It's not just the job, Dad. I did great things with our company's money, managed it to the penny, made them millions, even billions, but did a crappy job with my own. I went to see a financial advisor not too long ago, and he told me not only can I not retire in 10 years unless I am able to save a lot more money, but he also took a look at my current financial picture and said I have about two months of runway before I have to take drastic action, whatever that is. I haven't figured it out yet. I don't want to go there." David was laying all his cards on the table. "Then Meghan's college is looming ..." David trailed off. That was the part he felt the worst about, lately. His daughter had worked so hard, got excellent grades and now here he was, unable to give her the one thing she really wants. College at UCLA.

Ron had never seen his son like this. David had always kept up appearances. Strong, confident, maybe even a little arrogant. Ron now realized the truth. He had kept up appearances about his marriage—that was a surprise to Ron, too—and now about his job and financial situation. That's why he and his son had drifted apart. Staying close took too much honesty. Through the years it had become clear. Ron didn't really know his own son anymore.

Chapter 26

Everything was always, "all good" when Ron asked David what was going on. Too many "All good's" and you can't help but feel disconnected. In a strange way, Ron was grateful to be let in his son's life. He had stories from his past where he felt lost, just like David was feeling now. Stories he never got to tell. You don't tell a 20-year-old kid those kinds of things. *I missed out on his thirties, forties and half of his fifties. Maybe it's time to talk like I never could before,* Ron thought. *It might be a risk. But what do I have to lose?*

"You know, David, there was a time in my life when I, too, felt lost. A few times, actually," Ron began.

"Yeah, but just look around. You've made so many smart moves in this canyon, Dad. I don't remember you ever missing a beat. You've always had everything figured out," said David, realizing for the first time, perhaps, that his own dad's seemingly perfect life was just too hard to stomach during those years when David's marriage was in trouble, when he was battling at work, when he was struggling to keep up with his friends and their increasingly lavish lifestyles. *Dad had to be looking down on me,* he imagined, *during those years. Even right now. His life seems simple and fulfilling. And mine is complex, getting more complex, and not at all satisfying. Dad has to be shaking his head wondering where he went wrong with me.*

"David, there's one big benefit of being old. By this point in your life, you've figured more things out—the hard way. Nobody gets to figure things out the easy way. Not even sure what *easy* is." Ron noticed that David was still looking down, not ready to make eye contact. "My smart moves were usually the last ones in a series of bad moves. Things that I tried that didn't work."

"You always had this place as a safety net," David interrupted.

"A safety net? A burden. When I was in my 20s and I had gotten back from military duty, I had seen some of the world. My buddies were going off to college on the GI Bill. But me, I was here. Couldn't leave my dad. He needed my help. I felt trapped. What could I do? I was all he had?"

David looked up, "This is a pretty great place to be 'trapped,' Dad." For the first time, David revealed how he felt about this homestead. "I mean, people travel here from all over the world. They vacation here."

"They do now. But then, it was just a backwater dot on the map. And, while all my buddies were making something of themselves, I was mending fences, cleaning out chicken coops ... it was a real low time in my life."

"I didn't know," David said quietly.

"Eh, these are things I haven't thought about in a long time. The difference was I eventually saw the possibilities in this place. I started to see what my own father didn't. I started taking ownership. And whether he liked it or didn't—sometimes he didn't—I started making a few changes. Adding a cabin or two. Replacing trees in the orchard. And just getting the place in shape and looking nicer for people passing through the area," Ron said. "The real big change was when I dusted off the old cider press." Ron had a smile on his face that bordered on a grin.

"What?" David asked wondering why his expression had changed from serious to reminiscent.

"Oh, I was just thinking about all the mistakes I made before actually getting a decent cider product out the door. You think I made only good moves. Before I learned how to press and store and sell cider, I lost entire harvests. Cider that turned hard and unsellable. Gallons upon gallons of it, just poured into the ground. Those were big loss years, and by that point your grandfather was gone. This was my income. It wasn't easy."

David was shocked. He had never known his dad ever had financial worries. He always thought that the worst part of running this place might have been the back-breaking work. Never the systems and processes, the learning curve. Those were things David faced in his career. He couldn't help but feel more connected, knowing his dad had been through the same kinds of things he had.

"I'm sorry, this isn't about my old war stories. This is you telling me what's going on. I just wanted you to know that sometimes things aren't as they seem," Ron said.

"Why didn't you ever tell me about the harvests, the cider?" David was curious, wondering if avoidance ran in the family.

"Oh, I don't know. You were a kid. And we didn't really talk about things like that. And later, we didn't talk about business, we didn't talk much at all. You were busy doing big business things. This little orchard and its 18 cabins were small time. Guess I thought you wouldn't be interested. And it was a long time ago. Best forgotten," Ron said, feeling a little like perhaps he could have tried harder years ago.

"You're right. I probably wouldn't have been interested. I was busy trying my damnedest to climb that corporate ladder and feeling pretty full of myself most of the time. It's pretty humbling to get kicked off it." David was really revealing how he felt. "I thought I was somebody. Boy, was I wrong about that."

"You are more than somebody. Don't forget that. On the other hand I know how easy it is to get to feeling that way. Do you mind hearing another story?" Ron really hoped David would give him the go ahead and not shut down. He needed to hear this. "About five … no maybe it was eight years into working here at Orchard Canyon, I felt like we had the place in good shape. All the repairs had been done, we were actually having folks passing through regularly and staying at the place, the apples were selling, and the gardens were producing. Dad would raise a steer from time to time, then butcher it. With that and along with the chickens and the garden, we had no shortage of food. And we had a few hands who did a lot of the routine work. And we had money in the bank."

"Sounds perfect," David said.

"It was perfect. It was so perfect that I decided to take a job in town. Building some of the stores that were going up. I had dreams beyond here. One company, owned by a kid I had gone to school with, was looking for help. I liked to work with my hands so I thought, 'What the heck?'" Ron was shaking his head. "You have to remember, by now my army buddies were graduated from college. They had good jobs. They were in the cities. I was here ... still," Ron said.

"What happened?

"Well, it went great for a few years. I started as a laborer, then moved up to job superintendent. Then my high school buddy and I got to talking. He was going to be putting in a new development and he wanted me to be a partner in it. He liked my work, liked me," Ron continued and couldn't help but notice David's disbelief. He never saw his dad as anything but a guy who worked this orchard and little summer vacation hideaway.

"Did it work out? A lot can happen with a development," David asked, keenly interested.

"Oh yeah. It went up. I mean a lot of the original buildings have been rebuilt now—it was where all those stores are in the south part of town," Ron knew that David had been to that shopping area many times.

"Yes, I know where you mean," David couldn't believe his dad owned part of that prime real estate. It's worth a fortune today.

"We did all the planning and we had a lawyer draw up the deal documents. The day that I was going to sign them, Dad got sick. He just keeled over in the lower orchard. In those days, medicine wasn't what it is today. It took hours before he could be seen by a doctor. And even then, there wasn't much they could do. He had had a stroke. Lost the use of his left arm. Or most of it." Ron couldn't believe he was talking about this. It was a very hard time.

"You never signed the contract, did you, Dad?" David could feel the disappointment his father still felt.

"How could I? Dad needed me back here. My life would have been very different if I had signed on that dotted line."

"But not necessarily better, do you think?" David asked out loud, surprising even himself that he thought life in this canyon seemed pretty good. He didn't used to feel that way.

"Well, who's to know? Better is what you make of something. And I made the best of it, that's all. You have to. I had to. So you see, I too was on a ladder that was going places. And got kicked off it for different reasons. Maybe the men in this family are always eventually drawn back to Orchard Canyon."

David looked down at the ground again. Wondering how he could not have ever known this about his own father. How naïve he had been to think that just because this place is beautiful the minute you cross the creek and go through that narrow gate that everything is perfect here. Like problems don't exist, and that this is all his dad ever wanted out of life. How childlike and arrogant at the same time to think real problems and disappointments only happen to people like himself. Big city guys with big dreams and bigger wins, bigger losses.

"Look, you're going to be fine. You know a lot, you have a lot to offer. You just haven't found what's next. It'll show up. Speaking of showing up, Meghan and Mrs. Ritter are expecting us to show up for dinner. Hungry?"

"Yeah, I am." David truly was. It wasn't that misery loved company. It just was somehow comforting to see that his Dad had been through his own challenges and that he got through them. And maybe he was right, the men in this family are always drawn back to the canyon. They walked in silence, but deeply connected, to the house. It felt good. The honesty ... for both of them.

Chapter 27

CHAPTER 27

The heaviness of the conversation on the cabin porch fell away the moment David and Ron walked into the house. Dinner that night consisted of homemade pot roast with potatoes and a fresh green salad. Also featured? Mrs. Ritter talking about her grandchildren and how grown up they all are. "Where does the time go?" she wondered out loud. So did Ron. He couldn't believe he had let so much time come between him and his son. As much as he didn't like to see anyone struggle, he couldn't help but be grateful. *Maybe this is what it took to bring us back together.* He tried his best to pay attention to the conversation at the table, but it was the talk he and David had on that porch that swirled in his head.

Meghan was quite proud of the work she did in the kitchen. She made sure everyone knew that in addition to cutting every last carrot, she also helped with the surprise dessert, which, when served, made everyone find room for just one ... or two more bites. Homemade brownies with vanilla ice cream.

Meghan, hadn't really ever prepared anything in a kitchen, other than pour some milk over cereal, make toast, slide delivered pizza onto a plate, or open take-out containers. That was the extent of her time in the kitchen at her dad's house. Even at her mother's house, Susan usually got home so late from work that cooking seldom happened. Mrs. Ritter was surprised that Meghan had never chopped up a carrot for a salad. "Well, the salad comes pre-chopped in bags from the store," Meghan said. "My mom and me, we eat a lot of salads. We just open a bag, pour on the dressing, and that's it." Mrs. Ritter knew she'd quickly realize here at the dinner table that salad out of a bag was not the same as fresh. And sure enough. Meghan took one bite, looked at her father and said, "Dad, I'm going to make this salad for Mom. It's awesome. I'll make it for you, too."

"Keep the recipe a secret," Mrs. Ritter said jokingly. "Okay, well I guess you can show your mom how to make it." Everyone smiled. David, especially, was thankful for the lighthearted conversation.

"Gramps, I said 'What did you think of the salad?' It's like you didn't hear me."

"Sorry, honey. I guess I missed what you said. The salad? It's the best I've ever tasted," Ron said. Mrs. Ritter chimed in to say that she had shown Meghan how to make her secret vinaigrette dressing.

"It takes the exact right kind of vinegar and a spice that must remain unknown," Meghan said elongating the word 'unknown' like she was a sorcerer in a teen fiction novel. "Plus, Mrs. Ritter had some awesome stories about the Great Depression for my paper!" Meghan was so excited to have yet another story of what that time was like for people and how they got along. She then coerced her new Orchard Canyon friend to tell it again. The best part of all this was that for the moment she forgot about the "letters" waiting for her at home.

David couldn't help but hear himself in parts of that story. He was going through his own Great Depression right now. How impressive it was for a man like Mrs. Ritter's father to just pack up and humbly take whatever came his way. How interesting that that job, working on Hoover Dam, became the work that defined him. More so than any banking job he had. It became clearer to David that he was thinking too narrowly. He was taking the path of habit, not that path that was clearly before him. He was fighting it. He was fighting his future and it wasn't an even match-up. The future always wins, one way or another. You can't stay where you are.

Maybe there was a "Hoover Dam" for him. Maybe it was already in front of him. He still felt like he didn't have much to offer. The work at the bank that he had become an expert in wasn't something lots of companies needed today. It was not something that you could market as a skill. It was specific, technical, and very specialized. What else could he do? How do you apply a skill that has been replaced by an algorithm?

David could see now that, in fact, that was exactly what had happened. It's what had been happening for years, he just didn't want to see it. *The old hindsight being 20/20*, he thought. And he realized that being a small cog in a very big wheel separated him from the realities of business. His view was minuscule on a daily basis. He never had a chance to see the big picture. The work he did at the bank, he completed it and the bigger-picture people inserted it into the grander plan, a plan he never saw again. That was it. He felt completely separated from the broader view. He had a broader view. But was it real? He never got to see the Hoover Dam completed in his work.

You don't know how business works, David. You've been living an expert's life. You're good at one little thing. And that's it. David's little voice became an unwelcome guest at dinner.

"My dad," Mrs. Ritter was still talking, "didn't care that he never was much good with a hammer or nails, he used to say. He just knew he had to move on and he could learn. It turned out he started not with a hammer but with a pick axe."

"Imagine, that dam being dug with raw muscle and determination," Ron said aloud.

"I'm sure there was heavy equipment, whatever that meant in the '20s, but my dad didn't have the skills to operate it. He knew how to swing an axe, though. So he did."

That'll be you, David. You're back to square one, you-know-who added in his head.

David excused himself for a moment and went to the bathroom. He closed the door, looked in the mirror and said, quietly, but forcefully, "Enough. Enough of you." He splashed water on his face. Pulled himself together, took a deep breath, and went back to the table.

At that point, Meghan was more excited than ever, "Tell them, Mrs. Ritter, how once the foremen realized that your dad was good with numbers and money, he got a different job."

"Yes, that's exactly what happened. I mean what company doesn't need someone good with numbers? Business is money! So my dad quickly moved up and never had to pound rocks again. That's how we were able to save a little bit and buy some land down the road where the resort is now."

David needed to hear that. He really needed to hear that. "What business doesn't need someone good with numbers? You're right. Business is money." he repeated. "Mrs. Ritter that is an amazing story. I can understand why your father was proud. Proud of all of it."

As they started clearing the dishes and cleaning up, Ron caught David alone in the dining room. "I'm glad we had our talk out there."

"Yeah, me too." David replied. And then after pausing, "I mean it. I really am." They hugged for the first time in a very long time. Tears welled up in their eyes.

CHAPTER 28

The drive home from Orchard Canyon was pretty quiet. At least at first. David was processing not just telling his dad what was going on with his life, but also how good it felt to reconnect. It was unexpected. David didn't know his father as a man; he only knew him as a dad. And this time, with this visit, there was an adult connection he hadn't experienced before. It was comforting and at the same time a little weird. David hadn't let anyone in that close in a long time. Maybe ever.

Meanwhile, Meghan was gazing out the window listening to music and ignoring the texts that were coming into her phone. David could see it light up every so often, although he couldn't hear the ding of a message hitting her phone. Meghan was thankful for Mrs. Ritter and the stories she told. She was happy to be learning how to chop carrots. The reason, of course, was that she had completely forgotten about the letter waiting for her from UCLA. Now that she was alone with her thoughts, her apprehension was back and it felt overwhelming.

"What if I don't get in, Dad?" Meghan broke the silence somewhere around the Camp Verde exit of Interstate 17, heading back to Phoenix.

"What if you don't what?" David was lost in his own thoughts and barely heard her.

"What if I don't get in to UCLA? I so want to go there." That wistful, slightly whiny sound that Meghan seldom ever voiced told her dad she really did want this. She was not a whiny kid.

"Well, you'll find out in a while and then you can plan from there. You'll have options if that doesn't work out," David tried to reassure her, but understood what it felt like to have your heart set on something.

"No, Dad. I'm going to find out when I get home tonight. Mom said there are letters waiting for me. I didn't get a chance to tell you. She called me while you were with Gramps." She relayed that her mom wouldn't open the letters.

"It is something you have to do, opening those letters. Well, in about an hour and a half, you'll know." *This is real world stuff* David thought. He couldn't give the assurances of old, "I'm sure you got in. You're smart." He wasn't sure she got in. Lots of smart kids apply to college and don't get accepted. It's life. But inside, while David wanted nothing more for her to get into the school of her dreams, a part of him was wishing she had a change of heart and saw how good the in-state schools were in Arizona. They were top ranked. But nothing he could say would move the ball down that field.

Silence again.

Then, as they were entering Black Canyon, Meghan pulled her headphones off her head and said, "Hey, you and Gramps were out working for a long time. Is everything okay? Mrs. Ritter wondered if Gramps might have strained his back again."

"No, he is fine. We just got to talking." David didn't know how far he should take the conversation.

After a long silence that seemed longer than it actually was, David finally finished his thought, "I told him about my job situation. That's what we were talking about, so ..." his voice trailed off.

"'Bout time. When do you think you'll get something else?" Meghan asked, displaying her youth through her casual ease. One day she would understand, but not now.

Chapter 28

"I'm not sure, Meghan. I'm not clear on what I want to do next ..." David was cut short.

"Well, I know what I want to do. I want to work in fashion or fashion marketing, or fashion media and Los Angeles is the place I have to be!" Meghan blurted out. She was visibly nervous and thankfully not able to ask too many questions of her father.

As they rounded the turn to drop Meghan off at her mom's house, it was as if Meghan had texted Susan to say they were almost there. Susan was standing on the porch. "Did you text your mother and tell her we were a block away?" David asked in disbelief.

"I did. I texted her." Meghan was once again smarter and braver than her dad gave her credit for. "Mom, do you have the letters?" Meghan shouted as she was getting out of the car. David had barely stopped at the curb. Didn't even have the car in park before Meghan was bolting across the yard.

"Well, hello to you too, sweetie." Susan said jokingly. "I can't have my feelings hurt when I'm competing with acceptance or rejection letters from colleges."

"Hi, David," Susan yelled as he walked up the drive.

"I understand there is some big news pending. Hi, how are you?" David flashed a smile at his ex-wife.

Meghan looked frozen as her mother held out the envelopes. "Go ahead, take them. Which one will you open first?" her mom waved the envelopes from UCLA and ASU a little, kind of like bait. She already knew the answer to her question.

"This is it," David said. And then thought to himself, *In more ways than one. This is it, the moment I find out how much deeper this chasm that is my life gets. The thought of college tuition. Out-of-state tuition plus everything else was going to be at least $70,000 per year.* For the first time ever, the notion of student loans became real.

Meghan tore open the envelope from UCLA. Pulled out a sheet of paper and began reading:

Dear Meghan:

I am pleased to inform you that you have been accepted to admission at the University of California – Los Angeles ... (and then a shriek!)

Everything after that was a blur for all involved. Meghan finally read the rest of the letter after her shriek, after jumping up and down a hundred times, and hugging her mother and father. Then jumping up and down again, and fanning herself. She could barely talk.

Finally Susan asked, “What else does it say! What else does it say?”

But David didn’t really hear anything after the word “accepted.” He could only think, *This is it. The future is bearing down on me, like it or not.* In between intermittent pangs of fear, he was overwhelmed with happiness for his daughter. He may have missed achieving his own dream of reaching the moon and the stars, but Meghan was clearly on her way to living hers.

Megan’s next hour was a blur of texts to friends who of course were OMG-ing and almost immediately after that, firing off plans to visit Meghan in La-La-Land! This was going to be so completely “AWESOME,” they wrote over and over. That universal word that everyone uses to describe everything was flying around Meghan’s corner of cyberspace like autumn leaves in a wind storm.

David and Susan might not be together, but they had Meghan in common and both of them shared in the joy of their daughter growing up. “It is so hard to believe she’ll be going off to college,” Susan said to the wind.

"It is, isn't it?" The wind was David's audience, too.

Meghan quickly emailed Gramps in between the flurry of text messages and emojis.

"Hey, Gramps! Guess what???? I got in to UCLA! Wooooooo hooooooo!"

His response was nearly immediate,

"Well, of course you did. You are UCLA material and I never doubted you'd get accepted for a moment. Congratulations, Meghan. You earned it.

Love, Gramps"

"I should probably head to the house. I'll let you two plan out dorm rooms and furniture and all the other stuff girls do to prepare for college. I'm guessing you DO want to go to UCLA, Meghan? I mean just to be clear," David joked.

"Daaaaad, you know I do!" Meghan rolled her eyes and smiled, knowing he was joking.

"Okay. Juuuust checking. Juuuust checking." He headed for the car and waved at the two who clearly were going to log onto the UCLA website the minute David was gone. Once they got into the house they learned all they could about residence halls and student life and, and, and ...

Chapter 28

While he was driving in his car, he asked Siri on his iPhone, “What are the tuition costs at UCLA?” She answered with a webpage and a link that showed his $70,000 a year guess was about right. While he was driving, Susan and Meghan were talking about fashion and majors and ways Meghan could take her interests and make an exciting career of it all.

“Meghan, I always tell students and young professionals, intern while you’re in school and work for someone else when you graduate, just to get as much experience as you can. Do a lot of different things and don’t get pigeonholed. That’s the only way you’ll know what you like and what you don’t like. You’ll start to see the bigger picture,” Susan said, knowing she was getting a little ahead of herself. Meghan was still looking at dorm rooms and which one might be assigned to her.

“I’ll figure it out, Mom,” Meghan was distracted with the excitement of being accepted and the random texts from friends that kept flying in. Susan knew that what she said was true and that Meghan might be ready for that conversation in a year or two.

Another conversation Susan would save for the future was to encourage Meghan to look for ways to become her own boss. To work for herself. Susan had told many students who call her for guidance that, “Very few make their way to CEO of a major corporation. And those who get there seldom do because they are the brightest at what they do. They get there by being the best at knowing how to get to the top. That in itself is a skill. Know yourself and which game you'd like to win at." Susan wasn't a ladder climber; she was the best at her job.

Ladder climbing wasn't a game David played well either, despite his attempts. For a few moments Susan felt sad that David was doomed to middle management and still stuck at the bank. How miserable she would be if she were still in her role at the bank.

"Mom, look at this room!" Meghan interrupted Susan's career advice daydream. "I hope I get a room like this one. It's AWESOME!"

"Of course it is, honey. UCLA is going to be AWESOME!"

Chapter 29

CHAPTER 29

A few days later, Meghan had a day off from school. It was a teachers' in-service day, so Meghan was at her dad's house basking in the glory of her college-bound future. While browsing the IKEA website for dorm room must-haves, her phone rang. "Hi, Meghan."

"Hi, Mom."

"Hey, I know you have no school today and of course, figuring that college kids can always use extra spending money, can you help us with an urgent social media push? We could really use you here," Susan sounded a little frantic so Meghan knew her mom wasn't just being nice trying to channel her a few extra dollars.

"Sure. I can help," Meghan replied.

Chapter 29

"Okay, thanks. The sooner you can head over the better!" Susan added that last comment just to make sure Meghan knew this wasn't a leisurely ask.

"Dad, can I have your car? Mom needs my help at the office." Meghan shouted to the bedroom.

David was getting ready to hit the pavement and start making his future happen. He wasn't sure what he was going to do exactly, but since his future was clearly underway, he felt he needed to catch up. "Meghan, I need the car today, but I can drive you. Are you ready to go soon?"

"Yeah. I can leave now," she said as she texted her mother back.

David started to think, there is no need to hold the truth back from Susan any longer. This little office visit might be the perfect opportunity to casually tell her what has been going on. So much better than making a call and dropping the bomb, "Hi, Susan, this is David. Hey I've been meaning to call you. I've been out of work for two months with no prospect of anything on the horizon. Just thought you should know." The thought of it made his stomach turn. Dropping Meghan by Susan's office was fate operating in his favor, he thought.

David began backing the Beemer out of the garage as Meghan fastened her seat belt. "So I started to fill out the paperwork online about dorms and roommates. I'm not sure whether I want to let them match me up with a roommate or room with a friend from my class who is going to UCLA too. She's sort of a friend; we'd say hi sometimes, but I don't want to hurt her feelings."

"I'm not sure you want to start off in college worrying about someone else. Maybe she'll want to room with someone new, too. College is a time to meet new people, to invent or reinvent yourself. I don't think you have to feel pressured to room with anyone. This is a new beginning," David said. Then he heard his own words: a time to *invent* or *reinvent yourself ... a new beginning ...* His college wasn't like that. Was he talking to Meghan? Yes, but he was also talking to himself.

He started to realize that maybe he was looking at his own situation the wrong way. This was *his* new beginning, not a continuation of a life that was behind him. Why hadn't he seen that before? His view until this moment had been how to get back on the track of his life, not how to seize the opportunity and discover a new track entirely. To see new options. Were there any in front of him that he had been missing? For the first time, David was open to what was beyond his narrow view of the past. He continued to back out and saw just how small the view was in that rearview mirror he was gazing into. And when he turned the car around, how expansive everything looked through the windshield. That was his future: big, open, bright. His past, tiny, dim and distant.

He felt like he had found the glue he could use to craft his message to Susan. Instantly he felt his mood rising. His tone wasn't going to be the "poor-me" conversation he thought it might become. Some of the excitement he felt a while ago was back. But this time, that excitement was in him, not in the hopes of a job that wasn't real or a person who would solve all his problems.

"What are you going to be doing at the office today, Meghan?" David asked.

"I guess there's this social media push. Probably for the new season's designer lines. Mom said she needed my help." Meghan was used to being thrown into the office fray and doing her best with little direction. This is one reason Susan felt Meghan had the makings of a leader. That she was destined to be at the top of her own company, or maybe even Susan's one day.

"It sounds like you have a handle on what you'll be doing today. Is Mom pretty busy? I was hoping to have a few minutes to check in with her."

David just wanted to hear himself say that out loud. He didn't expect Meghan to say anything one way or the other. She wasn't like some kids who were all caught up in their parents being together. To her they seemed like they got along better now than they ever did when they were together. Nothing wrong with that, especially since that made her own life a lot less stressful.

David made his way onto the freeway and, while Meghan was texting her friends, he was running through the conversation he'd soon have with Susan. In all of this, he has been so focused on the outcome of simply "make my problems go away," that he hadn't even thought about the concept of "opportunity." He silently kicked himself for taking so long to arrive at this alternate view of his situation. Truth is, he wasn't even sure now what all that meant; he just knew this morning he felt different.

Susan's company headquarters were in a cool, retro historic building in the old warehouse area of downtown Phoenix. Lots of entrepreneurial businesses are in the area, including start up tech companies and ones that are further into their business growth trajectory like Susan's. David pulled into the parking lot and thought, *This place is so Susan. It has a good feeling. Like change is happening here. Innovation. Energy. Newness.*

He contrasted his current energized feeling to the feeling he would have when he'd pull into the underground parking garage of his old job. He used to work in one of the high-rise bank buildings several blocks north of Susan's building on Central Avenue. The minute he'd pass the guard gate, the status game started. Whose parking space is closer to the elevator? Whose parking space is on the ground floor? How far is your space from the top execs? Who got preferential treatment? And then, of course, who had the most expensive car, the newest car, the convertible. And how can he or she afford that?

All this negative energy would flood in every morning in a dark and dingy concrete basement for cars. "What was that about?" David unknowingly asked out loud, never before realizing this mind game was happening to him first thing in the morning and last thing in the evening, day in and day out.

"What was what about?" Megan asked.

"Oh, nothing. I was just thinking ..." David trailed off and slid into a bright parking space that actually had a view of South Mountain Park which is the biggest inner-city park in the world. Here he was, working downtown for so many years, and he never noticed the tens of thousands of acres of mountainous preserve directly to the south of the city. *I was in a basement,* he thought, *when everything new in the world was happening above ground. What the F?*

Meghan grabbed her pack and made her way to the front door with David following closely behind her. When they walked in, Kaylie, Susan's young "ambassador of first impressions" who wore jeans and a trendy top—both part of Susan's carefully-curated fashion line—greeted them with a smile, a warm "Hi!" and a hug for Meghan. "Go on back, your mom's ready for you. You know the way, right? I hope you're ready. It's crazy around here!"

And it was crazy. Designer samples were all over tables in the open warehouse workspace as Susan's team decided yay or nay on what they'd feature next season. Meanwhile the marketing team was glued to their computer screens posting, posting, posting images of the current line now in full scale launch and generating buzz on social media. Operations people were running from one place to the next making sure that orders were being shipped and returns handled. Even the customer service people who handled the complaints were upbeat and happy. Everyone was happy.

David looked around, taking it all in. For the first time, he actually believed work could be like this, because, guess what? Here it was, happening right in front of his face. And it had always been like this for Susan. He used to think, particularly when her company was smaller, that this culture was just a game. That it couldn't last. *Once this turned into a real business, Disneyland would be over,* David thought. He used to look down on the whole thing, like Susan's business wasn't a real business. The bank, on the other hand, was a real business.

Today, he felt differently. Clearly this *is* a real business. It's been a real business for several years now and maybe, just maybe, the energy here is a big reason for that success. Susan walked out of her office obviously having received a text from Kaylie saying she had guests.

"Hi, honey!" Susan said, giving Meghan a hug. "And David, nice to see you! To what do I owe this honor?" It had been years since David had actually walked into Susan's building. She could see the look of amazement on his face. *Is he surprised how big this is now,* she wondered. "Meghan, go see Alyssa right over there, she'll get you going. We've got sooooooo much to do to make our launch numbers and we're sooooo close," Susan glanced over to the chalkboard wall where some talented illustrator drew an eight-foot champagne bottle. "When the bottle is all colored in, that means we've met our goal! All that graffiti around it keeps us motivated."

David couldn't help but compare the bottle and the catchy, funny, and motivating sayings around it to the spreadsheets and occasional "goal thermometer" that would grace the break room at the bank. *That was night ... and this is day,* he thought. Pure daylight.

Chapter 30

CHAPTER 30

Meghan followed Kaylie to the work table she shared with the three social media associates she was in charge of. "Hey, everybody, you remember Meghan, right? Meghan, you remember this scrappy posse, right?"

"Yes, hi, you guys!" As she glanced around she noticed one of the team members was wearing a UCLA sweatshirt. "Hey, did you go there?" she asked looking at him directly across the table.

"Where? Oh, the sweatshirt! To UCLA, yeah, I did. Loved it! Go Bruins!" She was talking to a recent grad named Devin.

"Cool, I just got accepted there. I can't wait," Meghan had a big grin on her face.

"You're going to really like it. Totally fun, I mean it's LA, right? I ate a lot of ramen. I was lucky to get some scholarship money which helped, and I had a job on campus," he said.

"Yeah, I was thinking I need to look into scholarships. I have good grades. But not sure I'll get anything or not. And I would like to work, even if it's here, remotely."

"You should totally check into the scholarships. There's a lot of money available," Devin said.

"Okay you guys, Meghan, I have tons for you to do and if you're serious about that working remotely thing, let's talk about it," Kaylie said.

While all the UCLA talk was going on across the room, Susan invited David into her office. It wasn't really an office with walls. It was more like a corner of the main open space, with a few glass, barn door partitions that could be slid shut for privacy. Susan shut them. "So David, I was wondering if you could take a look at our year-end financial projections. I'd like to see if there's a better way of doing this, given all the news about new tax laws and everything. I have good advisors, but I'd like your eyes on it too. Is that okay?"

"Sure. Of course. I'm here, right?"

"Yeah, you're here." Susan hesitated before asking, "Mind if I ask *why* you're here? You normally just drop Meghan off."

"To help you, I guess." David started, feeling removed, his old defensive-self returning. Why did Susan always make him feel defensive, so competitive and put off? Then for the first time, his little voice didn't turn on him. It said, *It's not Susan. You do it to yourself.* David heard the truth loud and clear. He continued far more humbly, "And, Susan, I'm here to come clean on what's been going on in my life for the past few months."

"What's going on? Are you okay?" Susan's brows and face took on a worried look just like Ron's did. Then brightened at a second thought, "Did you meet someone?!" Susan has always wanted David to be happy, and if that meant finding a new love, all the better.

"No, no, nothing like that. I wanted to let you know that I haven't been working at the bank for a while. There was a merger and, well … I was a casualty of downsizing and automation. Truth is, I've been struggling to find another job, and struggling to even know what that next job looks like. What industry it's in … what I can do," David regretted adding that last bit to his confession. It sounded weak when he heard himself say it. But it was true. He didn't know what value he could bring to another company.

Big companies have a way of doing that. Workers get so pigeon-holed into one tiny area of a mammoth business that it feels impossible to apply those specific micro-skills to another job at another company. That leaves workers feeling incompetent, and fearful wondering if they'll ever find work again at the same pay level or above. David had heard plenty of others before him say that very thing. "Who would hire me? I don't really know how to do anything. No one wants what I do. Or, my skills aren't transferrable."

Susan was so lucky, or maybe just really smart, David had begun to realize. She got out before those corporate mind games made her feel worthless. She started her own business and in so doing became a generalist, learning from the ground up enough to lead a team of smart ambitious brand evangelists around here. They seemed to work with an enthusiasm well beyond that of typical employees. *That's probably what Edgar did at Blackstone Adventures,"* thought David.

"Geez, David. I didn't know. Why didn't you tell me? You gave a lot of years to that place. I'm so surprised they let you go."

"It happens. New people come in at the top. They don't know the history .... Or care to know it. And then, they bring in their friends and that's it," David said, seeing the reality and feeling like his burden of secrecy and ego had been lifted.

"Are you okay? What are you going to do? What are you doing?" Susan asked. She had a million questions. She was concerned. She knew how David could get. Lost in his own anger and self-doubt. That competitive defeat that played such a role in the break-up of their marriage.

"I think I'm better now. Like now, meaning today. Yesterday I wasn't as good. I had a bit of an awakening this morning. Along with that, it does feel good to come clean."

"You know you can always tell me things, David." Susan knew that he was still David and that meant always wanting to appear strong.

"No, I know. I know. But I hoped my unemployment would be short-lived. Now as time goes on I'm more confused about what my next move should be or will be. I don't mean to be a whiner, but I'm not sure what I know how to do."

"Are you kidding? You know finance!" Susan exclaimed. "I wish I knew finance like you know it!"

"Yeah, but I know just small parts of it, not the big picture," David said. He was trying to set the record straight.

"But David, your view, your experience is perfect for entrepreneurial businesses like mine. You were helping finance businesses like mine. That's why I wanted to talk with you. Because you see things I don't," she could believe in him because she knew David better than anyone. She did find it shocking, however, that someone with so much financial knowledge would feel at a loss for work. "David, you have to believe and then you'll see it."

"I've heard that before," David said, not knowing how to answer her. He didn't believe. That was his problem.

"Oh my gosh. In my world, the entrepreneurs I meet, they are cowboys. They know how to start companies, power through product development, and sell anything. But they are not the best money managers. They know enough about financing—with a few exceptions—to be dangerous. And that can be lethal to the health of their own businesses," said Susan.

She realized just how far apart their worlds had become. Hers in the fast-paced entrepreneurial warehouse and his still stuck in big bank corporate high-rises. "Entrepreneurs are always looking for smart trustworthy finance people to guide them and do the work they hate doing and aren't very good at. Just like I am today."

David just listened, not really sure the demand was as big as Susan was making it out to be. But then he thought about his own father and the cider business. How much of an untapped gold mine that was. His dad just didn't know where to go to get some financing help. Or maybe he knew where to go, but not how to evaluate a good opportunity from a bad one.

"You may be right, Susan. I'll think about it. What can I help you with today?"

Susan, when she got an idea, often didn't let it go. She was excited to think that David might be open to a whole new world. More exciting, and more within his control. That he might begin to feel the resurgence she now feels about her career and life and well, everything.

"Okay, the last thing I'll say," this was totally Susan and she knew David was thinking that. "The last thing I'll say is that you need to find and do something you love. Not something that is all about the money. Now is the time to really go with your passion. This is so exciting!"

“That’s a great thought, Susan. But I have used up most of my savings and Meghan’s college is approaching fast. I have to tell you, I’m stressed about it. So money unfortunately will have to be a big part of the equation.”

“All I’m saying, David, is that you may be surprised. What starts small can become very big very quickly, so long as you get up every morning and love it. Just look at me.”

He knew Susan was right. He could see it. And for the first time, he didn’t just toss her advice away. He knew she had his best interest at heart, and maybe she did see something in him he didn’t see in himself. Maybe there was a need for his skills. “I get it,” he said, but in truth he was just beginning to get it.

“Okay, I’ve preached enough. But I am really excited for you!” With that, Susan got out her reports and they began to review them.

CHAPTER 31

David's drive home was music-free, and almost phone-call free. The words Susan had said were circling in his mind. *Maybe there is a place for a person like me who knows financing, who can match money with financing needs, who can spot a good deal from a bad one and who could advise a whole new generation, heck, two generations of business owners that were sprouting up everywhere in Phoenix.* "What was I thinking?" David said to no one. "You weren't thinking. That's the problem. You were wallowing. You were letting fear get in the way."

Almost instantly, the tall bank buildings that he glimpsed in his rear view mirror looked like small distant relics of not only his past but the world's past. Just then, his cell phone rang. It was Susan. "Hey, what's up?"

Chapter 31

"Hi, David. So, I was thinking there's someone I want you to meet. I mean if you're open to it. He's one of my fellow business owner friends. We're both on the advisory board for the downtown homeless shelter. He could really use your help. He is looking to expand and has contacted a few investment banks, but he just doesn't know what he's looking at. Would you mind?"

Susan knew that this would be a match made in business heaven. She wanted David to experience his own value and she wanted her fellow board member who was trusting to a fault to not get taken to the cleaners.

"Sure. But I'm not sure how I can help him ..." David began, hearing himself and not liking it.

Thankfully, Susan interrupted, "Believe me, if you just meet with him and start asking him about what he is doing and what his goals are, you'll know how to help him. He may even pay you!"

"Okay. I'll talk with him. And he won't owe me anything." Susan texted David the number and David promised to call him once he got back to the house in Scottsdale. No sooner did David hang up the phone than the car in front of him swerved out of its lane to the right. David instantly knew why. In the lane sat a large rock about the size of a toaster that obviously had flown off of a landscape truck. David had no time to maneuver into another lane and his bad left tire hit it dead on.

The car jolted and a second later careened into the left lane. Drivers behind him slammed on their brakes and as if in slow motion, he began sliding into the left shoulder of the freeway toward the wall. Somehow, by some miracle, none of the cars behind him made impact with him or each other. But as he began to roll to a stop on a shredded tire with six lanes of 75-mile-per-hour traffic whizzing by, he sat in his car and wept.

He was shaking, terrified and thankful. What if Meghan had been in the car? He was thankful that no one got hurt, that the blowout didn't cause a high-speed chain reaction, and he was grateful that he was okay. He also wept because he realized just how quickly life can be taken away. How precious it is and how foolish of him to be trudging through it. Turning small hurdles into what seemed like massive, unsolvable problems.

Phoenix is a friendly city, so it didn't take long before another driver pulled up behind him to see if he was okay. David wiped his face quickly and rolled down his window. "Hi, there."

"Wow, I saw that from the overpass and you're lucky to be dent free and I don't mean your car. Are you able to change this tire? You look shaken up. Let me help and we'll get it done quick."

David took a deep breath and said, "Yeah, let's get this tire changed. Thank you. Thank you for stopping. That really did shake me up."

The man was right; it took all of about 15 minutes for David to be on his way. He got the man's name 'Stu Reynolds' and contact information. He wanted to send him a note or something for all his help. People do look out for each other in Phoenix and Stu made David think he, himself hadn't been doing enough of that. The last few months he was so wrapped up in his own problems that he couldn't see anyone else.

Thanks to Stu, when David got home—he stopped and got four new tires first—he called Susan's friend. Why let any more of life go by? And rather than immediately trying to find out how her friend could help him, David took Stu's stance of: How can I help you?

David was shocked. The call went so well. It was the first time he didn't feel competitive with a business person. It was the first time he felt relaxed and just listened. Like Stu, when the time came to contribute, David did it effortlessly, sharing what he knew and suggesting next steps. Before David knew it, Susan's friend was feeling more confident, and so grateful for David sharing his knowledge.

"I'd love to have you come by my business, I'll give you a tour. I have a feeling there are a lot of other things I don't know. Ever have that 'don't know what you don't know' feeling? I have it right now," and then chuckling asked, "Would you be game?"

"Of course, I'd be happy to. I'd enjoy seeing what you've built," said David. The info exchange took place and on a day of so many firsts, David was for the first time in a long time feeling part of the business game again. It was a first step, but it was a step. And it felt really good. Business, he was starting to realize, happened in a lot more places than just the high-rise buildings. This felt like real business.

Despite the trauma of the high-speed near miss, David felt optimistic. He got up from his desk and walked through the hallway. He stopped and looked at his reflection in the mirror hanging on the wall and said, "This was a good day." And he meant it. Another first.

Chapter 31

CHAPTER 32

"Meghan, are you ready for your dress rehearsal tomorrow?" David was talking about the presentation of her senior project she had planned for Gramps. "We'll be leaving for Orchard Canyon tomorrow morning around nine a.m. Dad and I want to get a jump on some fence repairs and I want to take another look at that old cider press and the big storage barn next to it." David had some ideas for that space and for what he thought it could really become: a full-fledged cider business and tasting room.

In the week since he talked with Susan, met Stu along the side of the road, and counseled Susan's friend, David's mind had been spinning. He spent several days assessing his current financial picture, and while it was no better than it was a month before, he didn't let it get him down. Instead he started using some of the wisdom he had just shared with Susan's business colleague on his own "business."

He arrived at a few realizations. The first one was that if he didn't get a job with a company he could work from anywhere. In fact, if he continued to work as a consultant—he already got a referral from Susan's friend—he wouldn't need an office. He could work from his home.

Another awakening was with Meghan leaving for college, he didn't need to stay in Scottsdale. If he could work anywhere, he could live anywhere. Even Sedona. And if he lived in Sedona, he just might be able to talk his dad into letting him expand the cider business. The demand was certainly there, but the supply wasn't. David knew how to fix that. And the employees Ron had running the orchard knew the ins and outs of production. David felt sure he could arrange for financing.

The third awakening was that David had a beautiful house. It was in a highly desirable neighborhood. After a little research he discovered AirBnB and VRBO rentals in his area were going for more than $800 per night, $3,500 over the weekend and over $6,000 per week. David started to think that if he rented his house even one week out of the month, his mortgage was more than paid. Rent it out for two weeks and he'd be cash flow positive. He planned on spending more time at Orchard Canyon anyway.

The fourth awakening came from Meghan. She told him about her quick chat with Devin, the recent UCLA grad. She said she planned on applying for some scholarships and David was all for it. "Why shouldn't my kid get rewarded for her excellent grades?" That made him hopeful that the next four years might be less of a strain.

"Dad, you know I am ready. I've been working on this project forever. My report is written, the PowerPoint and even an online video that goes with it are done. It's going to be awesome!"

David was so proud of his daughter. She never took the easy way out. Even though she was a typical teenager; texting constantly; chatting about this friend or that; and stressing about hair, clothes, shoes, makeup, when it came to her work, she was focused and in it. Her results showed. Meghan was going to graduate at the top of her class in just a few months.

How did I lose that dedication and belief in my own life? David wondered. *How did I forget that I had dreams worth going for? I used to shoot for the moon. How did I lose that feeling, that good feeling, that came from achieving? Why did I give up on my dreams—of being an astronaut, of literally going to the moon—so quickly?* He knew the answer. Because he followed "the path" everyone took, and the path turned out to be a lie. Or at the very least, not as relevant or reliable as it used to be.

David was beginning to see that veering off the path was where reward lived. Blazing your own trail and working it hard got you further than following in step with everyone else who were hoping, working, competing and clawing to excel and win at everyone else's expense. He was quickly learning that when you open your mind to reinvention, the world looks very different. It appears bountiful and full of opportunity, not scarcity. There are no job issues; you create your job.

There's almost too much opportunity! Where David once saw no future for himself, he saw three or more: the rental of his home, the cider business at Orchard Canyon, and his finance consulting business. Each one equally as exciting as the next. He thought about his bank buddies, the one he met for drinks a few months ago and he actually felt sorry for him. *He doesn't see it. He doesn't see the world of abundance at the feet of seemingly rarified skyscrapers.* They are not rarified. They are relics, and David caught himself in the nick of time. Before he became a relic himself.

David heard his phone buzzing. Looking around his desk it was buried under all his planning notes. “Hey, how’s it going, Susan?”

“Hi, David. I was just calling because my entrepreneur friend is ecstatic with the help you gave him. He’s going to call you on Monday and offer you a consulting gig! Isn’t that great news?” Susan was so happy for the both of them.

“Well, that is beyond great news. He’s a good guy and I do feel like I could help him grow his business faster and with less risk,” David said.

“See, I told you! You have this ability to see a business opportunity in terms of money. Most of us entrepreneurs, we see it in terms of products, or marketing, or innovation. Without your money mind, things can get scaarrrrry!” Susan said.

“You’re right, you’re right. Completely right,” David finally felt it.

“So you’ll do it?” Susan asked.

“What? The consulting work? Yeah, I’ll do it. Hell, yeah.” David was completely beside himself. If he got one or two of these clients he would be able to make two to three times his monthly salary at the bank. But he didn’t want to get too optimistic. Then Susan chimed in.

"Okay, great, because I have another friend I want you to meet. She needs your help too and you're going to love her."

David felt his heart race. His door, the door that was always there, was now in plain sight and opening fast.

Chapter 33

The next morning, Ron was outside as always when David and Meghan arrived. But this time they had another passenger with them. It was Susan! She managed to peel herself away from the fashion world and take time for a little R&R—Orchard-Canyon style.

"Is that Susan? Susan? My goodness, it is, it is! It is so wonderful to see you. It has been way too long," Ron said, looking her in the eyes and giving her a big hug. Then looking at her again, and hugging her again.

"Awww, Ron, it is so good to see you." She looked at Ron and then around the property, "My gosh, you look great! The place looks great! The cabins look full! You're a regular Conrad Hilton in this little canyon."

"That's what I said!" Ron and Susan both laughed and got everyone else chuckling too. David had forgotten how absolutely charming Susan could be.

"Hey, Gramps!" Meghan gave a quick hug and then made her way into the house to set up for her big presentation run through. Susan had to come and see it, but in truth, she really wanted to see Ron too. To reconnect a little. And now that David was seeing the world a little brighter, he was easier to be around. His energy was positive and Susan liked that.

"Well, c'mon in and we'll get you all settled." Ron, Susan and David grabbed a few things from the car and followed onto the front porch.

"This place hasn't changed a bit. Still warm and homey, still have CNN on the TV," Susan commented and laughed.

"Yeah, if you listen too hard to all that, the nation's going to hell in a hand basket. But I'm not worried. I got my friends, my family, my house, my orchard, and my little Hilton here in this canyon," Ron joked. But in a way, he wasn't joking. His friends and family had saved him during the low points in his life. And this land, the buildings, the businesses here in the canyon buffered him from the economic crises a lot of people faced through the years.

"And if I can talk you into it, you'll have a growing cider business," David said.

"Let's sit down and catch up. We'll have some coffee. A pot is already made."

As they got caught up on family milestones and local affairs, Meghan was setting up her computer for her big presentation about employment and life during The Great Depression. She plugged it into the back of the television and instantly CNN was gone and her opening video was all cued up.

"Okay, I'm ready!" she announced from the parlor toward the kitchen.

"I guess she's ready, Dad. We'll work on the fence after the big history lesson," David said and the three of them all got up with their coffee and marched according to orders, into the parlor.

Meghan started the video. She set to music historic clips of the stock market decline, people rushing the banks, the government food lines, and people hoping and praying for work. It was all very well done, emotional, and moving. "Wow, Meghan, you have a talent for this. Your video is really good."

It was really good. And it hit David pretty hard. He could identify with the hopelessness the people of that era had in their eyes. He had been where they were. He had seen it in his own eyes, unbelievable to him now. How could he have felt that way in our modern times where now, as he is beginning to see, opportunity is everywhere. He teared up because he was so thankful to Susan and Ron and Meghan for helping him realize what he had been missing. For opening his eyes.

"There's more to come!" Meghan said. She was glowingly proud.

When the two minutes of "stage setting" was over, Meghan began:

"If the 1920s were roaring in America. They were whimpering by the beginning of 1930. You see, the bottom fell out of the stock market and America entered into The Great Depression." Ron knew this scenario all to well. He remembered his dad teaching him about the three tiers of wealth: land, companies and paper. When things go downhill, the slide happens with paper or stocks first, and like so many times before the decline is swift, universal and catches people off guard.

"In 1931 more than 800 banks closed their doors because they didn't have enough money to pay the people who had savings account. Those people lost everything and never got their money back. A few months later, even more people lost everything.

The number of bank failures grew to more than 11,000. My own family who lived in Oak Creek Canyon in Sedona, hid money in their barn, probably because they didn't trust the banks." Meghan clicked to a PowerPoint slide showing the jar she found in the barn and where it was hidden. "This jar I found contained nearly $2,000! A fortune back then!"

"It was a true financial crisis, a social crisis and a personal crisis for millions of people. They lost their savings. The communities suffered. And many people lost hope, leading to emotional depression too." David felt like she was talking directly to him. He realized how much his own job loss negatively affected his savings, his business network, and his emotional stability. Great depressions, it seems, are happening every day.

"Many of the people affected by the crash had jobs and investments that afforded them a high standard of living. They attended parties," Meghan said as she cycled through slides of the lavish 1920's lifestyle. She continued, "They bought cars, they spent money on clothes, and more. They thought the good times would never end. When they did end suddenly, these people lost practically everything. Many didn't have enough money even for food. So the government helped out," Meghan flashed up more pictures of food lines and people in suit coats and hats along with immigrants in ragged work clothes together all looking for help.

While David was viewing images from the 1920's he was seeing his own life in the 2000s. He had been living a lavish lifestyle. His pricey home, high car payment, expensive remodel, every gadget that existed, boats, all these images running through his own mind. He had to keep up with the people he parked next to in the concrete basement tomb of his office. He never thought the money to pay for all these things would go away. He too was caught off guard. His consumerism, like the consumerism of the 1920s practically broke him. *Thank God Meghan didn't give this presentation a week or two ago,* David thought, *I may not have made it through!*

"My family lived through The Great Depression in Sedona. There they owned their land and on it was the apple orchard. No one owned any stocks so the market crash didn't exist for them. They had a big garden and it produced much of their food," she showed photos of the old homestead she had found in the attic of Ron's house. "And they had livestock which they raised and butchered for meat. What they didn't use, they sold and that gave them money at a time when jobs were scarce. It was this that formed the thesis of my entire project: That the people who were self-sufficient and could produce the basics that everyone needed and had more than one way to make money survived better during this tough time than the 'consumers' who solely relied on a paycheck, a single source of income, and produced nothing."

David thought, his ancestors didn't have an easy life. But it was a relatively predictable one. They owned their land, so there was no debt. And unlike the crisis that hit the farms during the depression, his family felt none of that. There was no crash in the value of this land and what it could produce for the family and the local community. He finally saw what Ron had been trying to tell him all along with the orchard, the resort, the cider business. What Susan was living with her business and her rental houses. And what Meghan discovered through her research. That stability comes from not one source of income, but many sources and a community that needs what is produced.

That's not the path most people learn about. They hear, "Go to school, get good grades, go to college, get a good job." That used to be all there was, but that has changed. People may get jobs but they don't last. We're all at the mercy of supervisors. There's no security in that. Individual crashes and depression can hit at any time.

Today, technology has led to boundless opportunities that are far more lucrative than the traditional path. And far more stable. His family has fared well by having multiple streams of income for generations during some very big ups and downs. Even the most recent Great Recession. Everything he was realizing over the last few weeks was becoming clearer and clearer.

David wasn't sure what kind of grade the teacher would give Meghan on her project, but to him it was an A+. It was a clarifying, affirming A+ in his own life. The three audience members were captivated.

Meghan went on to describe how the government stepped in and created programs to employ those in the food lines. She shared Mrs. Ritter's family story. President Roosevelt enacted the New Deal. And a few years later, the government created Social Security to create a safety net for the future. It created the Securities and Exchange Commission to monitor the dealings in the stock market and not long after that the Federal Bureau of Investigation. Ron couldn't help but notice the juxtaposition of those three government bodies. Each one checked the others, and each one fed off of the others.

Ron remembered his father saying that desperate times called for desperate measures. Around 1933, everyone had to turn in their gold currency and it became illegal to own gold. The government collected $300 million worth of gold and $470 million in gold certificates and paid people about $21 per ounce. Once all that gold was in the government's possession, the price was raised about 70 percent to $35 per ounce. That inflated the money supply and helped the government fund all these programs. "It was World War II that got us fully out of the Great Depression and made our country and its people the strongest in the world. It made us producers again," Meghan said.

Meghan concluded her report, "The lessons I learned by taking a step back in history, by looking at my own family's history is simply this. Downturns happen, as do upturns. No matter where you are, the people who get through the downturns best and the people who do the best in the upturns are those who own something of value, meaning it makes them money. Who have more than one way to make money. And who have a solid community around them that wants what they produce. Thank you."

Through the enthusiastic applause and cheers, David thought, *It takes a child to see the truth so simply. A truth that is easy to lose in the daily grind of life and pressure and rhetoric. This is what I needed to hear. I'm on it, excited about it, and grateful to you, Meghan.*

Chapter 34

CHAPTER 34

Meghan got an A on her senior project. And she changed a few lives with it as well — her father's, for sure. Yes, somehow Meghan was able to see what life tends to cloud. At her graduation she received her diploma with honors. David, Susan, and Ron were all there to celebrate her achievement.

As they sat around Ron's kitchen table a month later, remembering that moment, and her little wave at all of them when she was handed her diploma, they agreed, it was an unforgettable day. "She is an amazing kid. You have to be proud of her, and I'm proud of you for raising her. You both did an excellent job," Ron said.

"Thank you, but Dad, the influence you have had on her in the last year has been life-changing. I don't believe I have ever said thank you for that. So thank you."

"And in no time, she's off to UCLA," Susan said. "She went after those scholarships and got them. I didn't even have to help her much. How did she get so wise?"

"And bold," David chimed in.

"I think we know where she gets all that from," Ron said with a smile.

"Speaking of bold, and not to talk shop, but I'm going to be meeting with a grower tomorrow who says he can supply us with as many as 2,000 pounds of apples, of the same quality as ours—you know, Arizona-grown, organic, non-GMO—in three months. It's a bold move but we could double our cider business in one year. I've done the projections and I think the demand is there, Dad," David said.

"What about labor?" Ron asked.

"I've got it covered. We can run two shifts with the staff we have. I think it will work," David said.

A few months earlier, David and his dad partnered to start a new business called Orchard Canyon Cider House. And it was already showing signs of success. They converted the old apple shed into a tasting room after David rounded up some financing for the remodel. It turned out beautifully and not only was it bringing new visitors to Orchard

Canyon, the increased exposure boosted their wedding business, too. More brides wanted to get married among the apple trees.

Ron loved having David as a partner who could not only take the business he built to the next level, for the next generation, but also collaborate on what that looked like. David found he enjoyed the physical work and because he was spending more time at Orchard Canyon, particularly when his Scottsdale house was rented out to vacationers, he was eating better. He weaned himself off of fast food and had already lost 25 pounds. He still had more to go but he felt stronger than he had in years.

David's consulting business took off too. One client led to two more and soon David was helping six different entrepreneurs through coaching and consulting. One of them was Edgar Blackstone! He's about ready to take delivery of those two "birds" he needed thanks to David arranging the financing. He and Edgar along with his CFO are also in talks with the acquisition target in Page. Soon Blackstone Adventures will be doing excursions on Lake Powell, one of the most beautiful freshwater lakes anywhere.

To say that David was having the time of his life would be an understatement. He was living life, really living, perhaps for the first time. He was contributing and helping people. And he was appreciated. He felt a bit like a hero. Financially, he had tripled his old bank salary and started paying off all his debt. It felt good to clean his life up. It was time. Way past time. And his bank account was growing with multiple sources of income. Fear no longer ruled his life.

"Dad, that was another amazing meal. Thank you," David said. Although this time he didn't feel as much like a visitor as he did one of the hosts. Orchard Canyon was becoming like a second home to him.

"Yes, thanks so much," said Susan. "You know it's nice to be back here with the two Reynolds men. Why don't you let me clean up here and you two relax."

"Good idea. But, I'm going to take a walk out to the upper orchard and check on the irrigation," Ron said.

"I'll go with you," David grabbed his jacket. It was summer but evening in the canyon could be a little chilly.

As they walked, they noticed the indigo sky awash in stars. "There's nothing like night time here. Never seen as many stars as you see here," David said. "I've always missed that living in the city."

"Well, you had some pretty big sights on the stars when you were a boy," Ron said. "Whatever happened with that? You wanting to be an astronaut?"

"I let someone rob me of my dream, Dad. I remember it like it was yesterday. And then I got good at it, robbing myself of my dreams. But that's all over. I've found that dreamer side of me again. This time I'm not afraid to take the shot."

Just as David said that, the full moon crested over the canyon wall. It was beautiful and bright and it seemed so close like it was within reach. "There's your dream, son," Ron said.

David looked up. Then he looked at his dad. "Nah, that was my old dream, Dad. I don't have to go all the way to the moon. I landed on my dream when I was born. I just didn't know it. It's Arizona. It's Orchard Canyon. It's always been right here ... Right under my feet. Finally, at last, I see it."

They turned and silently walked toward the orchard, the moonlight guiding their way.

Best-Selling Books In the Rich Dad Advisors Series

BY BLAIR SINGER

Sales Dogs
You Don't Have to Be an Attack Dog to Explode Your Income

Team Code of Honor
The Secrets of Champions in Business and in Life

BY GARRETT SUTTON, ESQ.

Start Your Own Corporation
Why the Rich Own their Own Companies and Everyone Else Works for Them

Writing Winning Business Plans
How to Prepare a Business Plan that Investors will Want to Read and Invest In

Buying and Selling a Business
How You Can Win in the Business Quadrant

The ABCs of Getting Out of Debt
Turn Bad Debt into Good Debt and Bad Credit into Good Credit

Run Your Own Corporation
How to Legally Operate and Properly Maintain Your Company into the Future

The Loopholes of Real Estate
Secrets of Successful Real Estate Investing

BY KEN MCELROY

The ABCs of Real Estate Investing
The Secrets of Finding Hidden Profits Most Investors Miss

The ABCs of Property Management
What You Need to Know to Maximize Your Money Now

The Advanced Guide to Real Estate Investing
How to Identify the Hottest Markets and Secure the Best Deals

BY TOM WHEELWRIGHT

Tax-Free Wealth
How to Build Massive Wealth by Permanently Lowering Your Taxes

BY ANDY TANNER

Stock Market Cash Flow
Four Pillars of Investing for Thriving in Today's Markets

BY JOSH AND LISA LANNON

The Social Capitalist
Passion and Profits – An Entrepreneurial Journey

About the Author

Ken McElroy is an accomplished business owner, investor, and mentor to entrepreneurs worldwide. He's also the author of other business titles, podcasts, and videos that help people find their dreams and accomplish them. He currently lives in Arizona and spends time at Orchard Canyon, a resort property nestled in beautiful Oak Creek Canyon, near Sedona.